ARCHITECTURAL
DESIGN

November/December 2017
Profile No 250

3D-Printed Body Architecture

Guest-edited by
NEIL LEACH and
BEHNAZ FARAHI

ISSN 0003-8504
ISBN 978 1119 340188

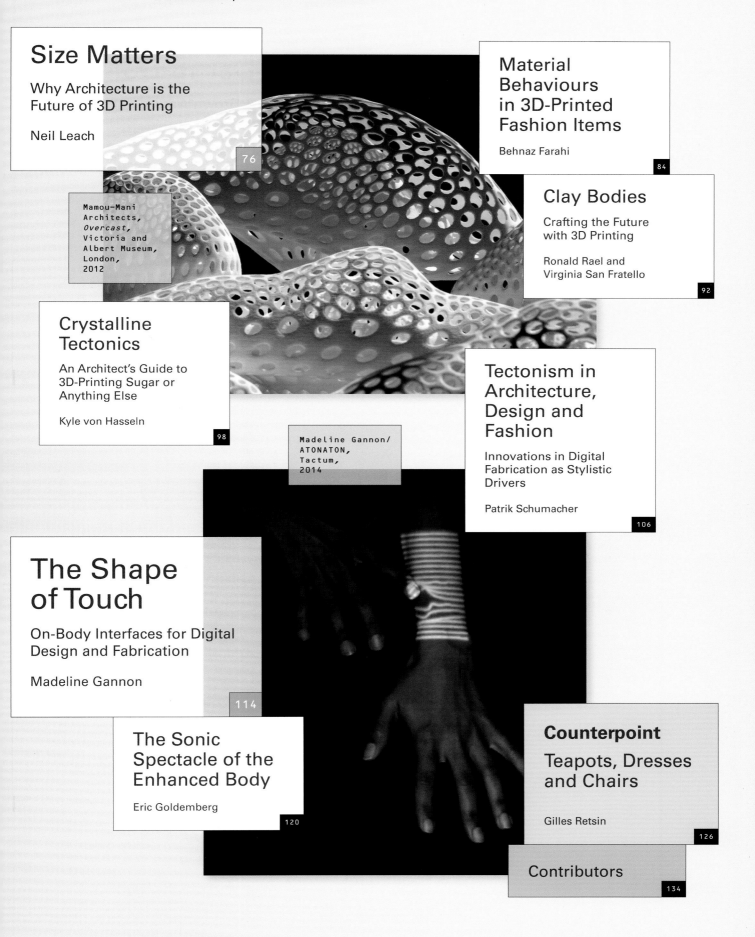

Editorial Offices
John Wiley & Sons
9600 Garsington Road
Oxford
OX4 2DQ

T +44 (0)1865 776868

Consultant Editor
Helen Castle

Managing Editor
Caroline Ellerby
Caroline Ellerby Publishing

Freelance Contributing Editor
Abigail Grater

Publisher
Paul Sayer

Art Direction + Design
CHK Design:
Christian Küsters

Production Editor
Elizabeth Gongde

Prepress
Artmedia, London

Printed in Italy by Printer
Trento Srl

Front cover: Behnaz
Farahi, *Caress of the
Gaze*, San Francisco,
2015. © Elena Kulikova
Photography www.
elenakulikova.com

Back cover and inside
front cover: Changhao
Xin, Bingmo Zhang and
Lingyu Wang, 3D-printed
wearable, College
of Architecture and
Urban Planning, Tongji
University, Shanghai,
2016. © Behnaz Farahi

06/2017

△⃝ ARCHITECTURAL DESIGN

November/December
2017

Profile No.
250

Disclaimer
The Publisher and Editors cannot be held responsible
for errors or any consequences arising from the use
of information contained in this journal; the views and
opinions expressed do not necessarily reflect those of
the Publisher and Editors, neither does the publication
of advertisements constitute any endorsement by
the Publisher and Editors of the products advertised.

Journal Customer Services
For ordering information,
claims and any enquiry
concerning your journal
subscription please go to
www.wileycustomerhelp
.com/ask or contact your
nearest office.

Americas
E: cs-journals@wiley.com
T: +1 781 388 8598 or
+1 800 835 6770 (toll free
in the USA & Canada)

**Europe, Middle East
and Africa**
E: cs-journals@wiley.com
T: +44 (0)1865 778315

Asia Pacific
E: cs-journals@wiley.com
T: +65 6511 8000

Japan (for Japanese-
speaking support)
E: cs-japan@wiley.com
T: +65 6511 8010 or 005 316
50 480 (toll-free)

Visit our Online Customer
Help available in 7 languages
at www.wileycustomerhelp
.com/ask

Print ISSN: 0003-8504
Online ISSN: 1554-2769

Prices are for six issues
and include postage and
handling charges. Individual-
rate subscriptions must be
paid by personal cheque or
credit card. Individual-rate
subscriptions may not be
resold or used as library
copies.

All prices are subject to
change without notice.

Identification Statement
Periodicals Postage paid
at Rahway, NJ 07065.
Air freight and mailing in
the USA by Mercury Media
Processing, 1850 Elizabeth
Avenue, Suite C, Rahway,
NJ 07065, USA.

USA Postmaster
Please send address changes
to *Architectural Design*,
John Wiley & Sons Inc.,
c/o The Sheridan Press,
PO Box 465, Hanover,
PA 17331, USA

Rights and Permissions
Requests to the Publisher
should be addressed to:
Permissions Department
John Wiley & Sons Ltd
The Atrium
Southern Gate
Chichester
West Sussex PO19 8SQ
UK

F: +44 (0)1243 770 620
E: Permissions@wiley.com

Subscribe to △⃝
△⃝ is published bimonthly
and is available to purchase
on both a subscription basis
and as individual volumes
at the following prices.

Prices
Individual copies:
£24.99 / US$39.95
Individual issues on
△⃝ App for iPad:
£9.99 / US$13.99
Mailing fees for print
may apply

Annual Subscription Rates
Student: £84 / US$129
print only
Personal: £128 / US$201
print and iPad access
Institutional: £275 / US$516
print or online
Institutional: £330 / US$620
combined print and online
6-issue subscription on
△⃝ App for iPad: £44.99 /
US$64.99

Guest-Editors Neil Leach and Behnaz Farahi have been collaborating since meeting at the University of Southern California (USC) where from 2011 to 2013 they worked on a research project to develop a robotic fabrication technology for 3D-printing structures on the Moon and Mars, funded by two NASA Innovative Advanced Concepts grants. Leach is an academic and theorist. Farahi is a creative designer and technologist. Both are trained as architects. This issue of △ illustrates their complementary perspectives on the new possibilities opening up for architectural designers within the emerging field of 3D-printed body architecture.

Neil Leach teaches at Florida International University, at Tongji University in China, and at the European Graduate School in Switzerland. He has also taught at many of the leading schools of architecture, including the Architectural Association (AA) in London, Harvard Graduate School of Design (GSD), Columbia Graduate School of Architecture, Planning and Preservation (GSAPP), Cornell University and the Southern California Institute of Architecture (SCI-Arc). He studied architecture at the University of Cambridge, and holds a PhD from the University of Nottingham. He is a licensed architect in the UK, and one of only three architects to be elected to the Academia Europaea. He has published over 30 books, and has guest-edited two previous issues of △: *Digital Cities* (2009) and *Space Architecture: The New Frontier for Design Research* (2014). His publications on architectural theory include *Rethinking Architecture* (Routledge, 1997), *The Anaesthetics of Architecture* (MIT Press, 1999), *Millennium Culture* (Ellipsis, 1999) and *Camouflage* (MIT Press, 2006). His publications on computational design include *Designing for a Digital World* (Wiley, 2002), *Digital Tectonics* (Wiley, 2004), *Machinic Processes* (China Architercture and Building Press, 2010), *Fabricating the Future* (Tongji University Press, 2012), *Scripting the Future* (Tongji University Press, 2012), *Robotic Futures* (Tongji University Press, 2013) and *Swarm Intelligence: Architectures of Multi Agent Systems* (Tongji University Press, 2017). He is also the translator of Leon Battista Alberti, *On the Art of Building in Ten Books* (MIT Press, 1988).

Behnaz Farahi is a creative designer and technologist working at the intersection of fashion, architecture and interaction design. She holds a Bachelor's and two Master's degrees in architecture, and is currently an Annenberg Fellow and PhD candidate in Interdisciplinary Media Arts and Practice at the USC School of Cinematic Arts. She is interested in exploring the potential of interactive environments and their relationship to the human body through the implementation of emerging technologies in contemporary art/architecture practice. Her goal is to enhance the relationship between human beings and the built environment by following design/motion principles inspired by natural systems. Application areas include architecture, fashion and interaction design. She also specialises in physical computing, sensor technologies, additive manufacturing and robotic technologies. Her work has been exhibited internationally at Ars Electronica in Linz, Austria; Context Art, Miami; the 3D Printed Fashion Show/Exhibition for Lexus x Voxelworld Show, Düsseldorf; and the Wearable Fashiontech Festival, La Gaîté Lyrique, Paris. It has also been featured in several magazines and online websites including *Wired*, *Frame*, the *Guardian*, BBC and CNN. Awards include the 2016 Innovation by Design Linda Tischler Award and the 2016 World Technology Award (WTN), and she is the recipient of a Madworkshop grant and the Rock Hudson Fellowship. She has also been an Artist in Residence at Autodesk Pier 9 in San Francisco. △

INTRODUCTION

NEIL LEACH

Synthesis Design + Architecture,
Durotaxis Chair,
2014

Multi-material 3D-printed chair inspired by
the biological process of the same name,
which refers to the migration of cells guided
by gradients in substrate rigidity.

WHAT IS 3D-PRINTED BODY ARCHITECTURE?

Let us start with a brief definition: '3D-printed body architecture' could be defined as 3D-printed designs by architects for clothing, shoes, food, chairs and other items either for the human body, or at the scale of the human body.[1] While the term itself is new, it nonetheless builds upon a number of existing traditions – the relatively recent history of 3D printing, and the longer-standing history of exploring the relationship between the human body and architecture.

Body architecture introduces a new genre of design practice to the rapidly expanding field of 3D printing, or 'additive manufacturing' as it is also called. The use of 3D printing for the fabrication of models has become widespread even within architectural education, to the point that Florida International University has invested in the provision of over 30 MakerBot 3D printers so that every student in its Innovation Lab is provided with their own personal machine.[2] Meanwhile, certain architectural practices, such as Foster + Partners, have been involved in exploring the potential use of 3D printing in building construction for both terrestrial and extraterrestrial environments.[3] Likewise, certain schools of architecture, such as the Institute for Advanced Architecture of Catalonia (IAAC), have also been conducting research into the potential of large-scale 3D printing.[4] 3D-printed body architecture is now opening up and expanding this tradition into a new design arena that shifts the focus from actual buildings to the household items to be found in them.

Behnaz Farahi,
Bodyscape,
2016

This 3D-printed outfit was designed according to a spiral logic based on the Langer lines of skin tension in order to allow it to flex with the body.

Caryatid statues,
Acropolis,
Athens,
2008

According to Vitruvius, the Caryatids represent the women of Caryae, who were punished for betraying Athens and siding with the Persians in 480 BC.

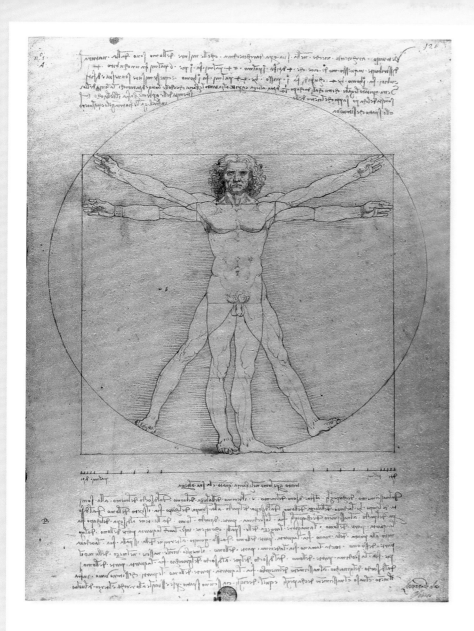

Leonardo
da Vinci,
Vitruvian
Man,
c 1490

This famous
drawing is based
on Vitruvius's
description of the
ideal proportions
of the human
body that were to
become replicated
in the design
of buildings
throughout the
world.

Body architecture also introduces a new perspective on the history of the relationship between the body and architecture. From Vitruvius's discussion of proportions in his treatise *De architectura* (*c* 30–15 BC),[5] made famous by Leonardo da Vinci's drawing *Vitruvian Man* (*c* 1490), through to Le Corbusier's stylised universal human figure the Modulor Man (1943), there have been attempts to relate buildings to the proportions and physiognomy of the human body. In the case of the Caryatids, where human figures serve as columns to support the entablature of the Erechtheion on the north side of the Acropolis in Athens, architecture literally takes the form of the human body. More recently, the connection between architecture and the body has led architects to develop an interest in the fashion industry, as in the 2007 'Skin + Bones' exhibition at the Museum of Contemporary Art (MOCA), Los Angeles, and the accompanying publication,[6] which drew extensively on architects designing fashion items. Body architecture draws from this in new and exciting ways to include not just fashion items, but also other design products for the human body.

So what are we to make of the emergence of 3D-printed body architecture? Does it constitute a passing fad where architects are merely experimenting with a new technology? Or could it perhaps be described as a form of 'proto-architecture' – like furniture, espresso makers and pavilions in the past – where architects explore at a smaller scale design strategies that will eventually feed into full-scale buildings? Or does it actually constitute a radical new genre of architectural design that not only expands the range of potential commissions for architects, but also forces them to rethink the very nature of architectural education and practice?

However we might appraise the work, one thing is abundantly clear: the contributors to this △ have all experienced some form of architectural education. In other words, the work is connected fundamentally to the discourse of architecture. The issue seeks to chart and analyse 3D-printed body architecture, and expose it as one of the most exciting developments in the discipline in recent years.

OTHER ARCHITECTURES

In few other disciplines are students taught to design, think three-dimensionally and understand material behaviour quite as well as in architecture. The skills taught in architectural education are readily transferrable to other arenas, and there has been a long tradition of architects migrating to other disciplines. Constance Adams, for example, studied architecture at Yale University, but moved into the space industry to become one of the designers of the International Space Station.[7] Joseph Kosinski, who studied architecture at Columbia University's Graduate School of Architecture, Planning and Preservation (GSAPP), moved into the film industry to become the director of movies such as *Tron: Legacy* (2010) and *Oblivion* (2013).[8]

Architectural education now places a heavy emphasis on digital skills. Moreover, with the introduction of digital technologies, as Mark Burry has noted, the differences between architecture and other disciplines are being effaced.[9] With these new opportunities has come an increase in the number of architects shifting to other design fields, especially 3D printing. For example, many have used their digital skills to work for fashion designers, such as Iris van Herpen, even though – or perhaps because – Van Herpen herself does not possess those same digital skills. In this issue of Δ alone, contributors Niccolò Casas (pp 34–9), Neri Oxman (pp 16–25) and Julia Koerner (pp 40–47) have all worked for Van Herpen, whether or not their names appear on the list of credits. Other contributors designing 3D-printed fashion items include Francis Bitonti (pp 64–9), Jessica Rosenkrantz and Jesse Louis-Rosenberg, cofounders of design studio Nervous System (pp 48–57) and Guest-Editor Behnaz Farahi (pp 84–91).

Often these designers engage with other computational systems. Farahi combines her interest in 3D printing with interactive systems. Similarly, Eric Goldemberg's MONAD Studio has collaborated with interactive designer Anouk Wipprecht on the design of a series of interactive 3D-printed musical instruments and a prosthesis for bionic pop artist Viktoria Modesta (pp 120–25). Meanwhile, Madeline Gannon explores how digital technologies can scan the topography of the body so that jewellery can be customised for the user (pp 114–19).

MATERIALITY

It could be argued that whenever architects find themselves working in other design fields, they always bring with them deep-seated architectural concerns, such as an interest in materiality and material behaviours. This is reflected in many of the contributions to this issue. Neri Oxman has been a leading figure in exploring the limits of 3D printing, and her contribution includes designs for 3D-printed glass (see pp 31–33). What distinguishes Oxman's work in particular is her capacity to marry technical expertise with design ability. Not only are the 3D-printed glass designs she has produced with her Mediated Matter Group at the MIT Media Lab technically innovative in their production methods, but the results are also ravishingly beautiful.

Farahi is likewise interested in 3D-printing materials, but for different reasons. Her article (pp 84–91) explores how design and geometry can be used to produce flexible items out of rigid materials, where printers using soft, flexible materials are not available or too expensive. Bitonti addresses similar concerns in his article (pp 64–9).

Emerging
Objects,
Twisting
Tower,
2017

This container
is 3D-printed in
salt from the San
Francisco Bay.

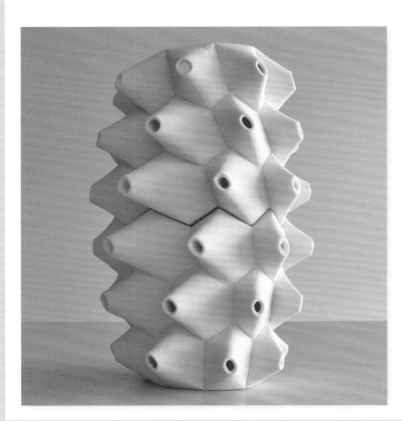

3D Systems
Culinary Lab,
Banana,
2016

This exploration
in 3D printing with
sugar takes the
form of bananas.

One of the key constraints with 3D printing is the cost of materials. Ronald Rael and Virginia San Fratello have been researching alternative low-cost materials, such as salt and clay.

One of the key constraints with 3D printing is the cost of materials. For some time now, Ronald Rael and Virginia San Fratello have been researching alternative low-cost materials, such as salt and clay. Their article (pp 92–7) explores the potential use of clay – one of the most ancient building materials – in one of the most contemporary modes of fabrication: 3D printing.

As a student of architecture at the Southern California Institute of Architecture (SCI-Arc), Kyle von Hasseln experimented with 3D-printing food. Together with his partner, Liz von Hasseln, he went on to establish a company for 3D printing with sugar, the Sugar Lab, which was subsequently acquired by 3D Systems. With a background in the sciences prior to his architectural education, for him the crucial challenge here is to understand the crystalline tectonics of sugar itself (pp 98–105).

The question of tectonics is also touched upon by Patrik Schumacher, Director of Zaha Hadid Architects (ZHA), which has produced a range of 3D-printed items, from jewellery through to relatively large-scale structures (pp 106–13). Schumacher sees his notion of 'tectonism' as a subset of the new global style that he has coined 'parametricism'. The extent to which tectonic principles can be understood within a framework of 'style' will no doubt generate considerable debate.

ECONOMIC MODELS

What is remarkable about the contributors to the issue is that, rather than working for others, many of them have seized the chance to set up their own 3D-printing design companies. As such, 3D printing presents a new field of potential entrepreneurship for architects.

Bitonti, and Rosenkrantz and Louis-Rosenberg have respectively established highly successful design practices, Studio Bitonti and Nervous System, focusing exclusively on 3D-printed wearables. Ronald Rael and Virginia San Fratello are the cofounders of 3D-printing 'make-tank' Emerging Objects. Likewise, Rem D Koolhaas, nephew of the famous architect with the same name from the Netherlands, has established his own shoe brand, United Nude, and collaborated with a series of architects in developing 3D-printed footwear (see pp 70–75). Julia Koerner has established JK Design, where she designs 3D-printed fashion items alongside buildings and products (pp 40–47).

Perhaps the biggest entrepreneurial success story, however, has been that of Steven Ma (pp 58–63), who trained as an architect at SCI-Arc, and has established a thriving 3D-printing practice, Xuberance, in Shanghai, where he designs everything from jewellery to architectural facades. Ma has been valued at $40 million by his investors, and has opened up a 3D-printing museum and three 3D-printing cafes in Shanghai.

FabUnion,
3D Printed
Chair,
2017

The chair is fabricated by robotic 3D printing with the colour change achieved by varying the mixing rate of the two different materials during the printing process.

WHAT IS ARCHITECTURE?

If architects are so successful in the domain of 3D-printed body architecture, as a result of their background training and skill set, then the question arises as to whether we should be reconsidering the very definition of architecture. For what begins to emerge is a portrait of architects as being defined less by their traditional roles within the construction industry, and more by a certain creative outlook and design sensibility that could be deployed in other industries.

'Are shoes architecture?' asks Koolhaas. Zaha Hadid, who collaborated with him in developing a pair of 3D-printed shoes, could certainly see the connection: 'Fashion and architecture can be considered as components within a single system of design. The immersive experience of a building can be likened to the tactile sensations of wearing a garment or an accessory. Just as clothing is based on the proportions of the human body, architecture must also be structured in relation to the human scale' (p 75).

As the Senior Curator of the Department of Architecture and Design at the Museum of Modern Art (MoMA) in New York, Paola Antonelli, herself trained as an architect, is in a unique position to offer an overview on these developments. Importantly, for Antonelli, design is everywhere, and architecture itself is an aspect of design. As she notes in my interview with her on pp 26–33 of this issue: 'It doesn't make sense any more to distinguish design disciplines because of the materials that they use, the dimensional scale that they tackle, or other old-school kinds of criteria.' As such, both architecture and 3D-printed body architecture fall under the category of design, and should not be distinguished in terms of scale.

Architecture and 3D-printed body architecture fall under the category of design, and should not be distinguished in terms of scale.

Arpi Mangasaryan, 3D-printed jewellery, Dessau Institute of Architecture, Anhalt University of Applied Sciences, Dessau, Germany, 2016

The jewellery was produced by Master's student Arpy Mangasaryan in a Body Architecture workshop tutored by Behnaz Farahi and Karim Soliman.

Changhao Xin,
Bingmo Zhang
and Lingyu Wang,
3D-printed wearable,
College of
Architecture and
Urban Planning,
Tongji University,
Shanghai,
2016

This item of apparel was
produced in a 3D-Printing
Body Architecture workshop
tutored by Behnaz Farahi
and Neil Leach.

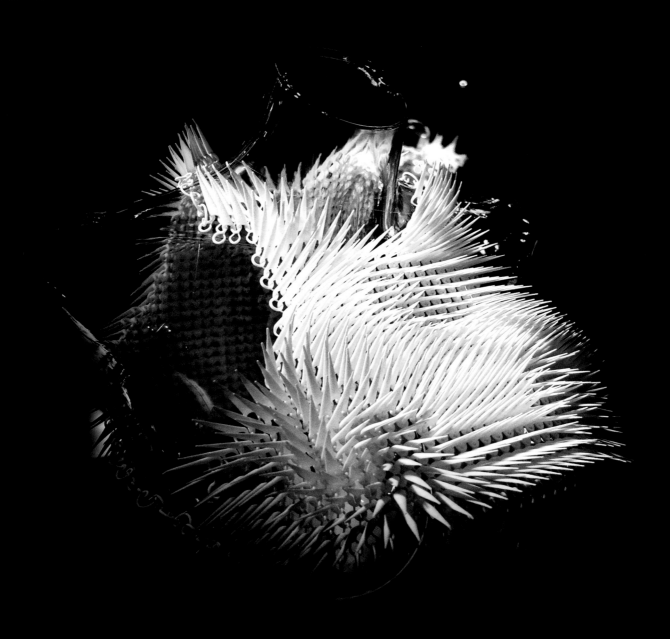

Ron Arad for pq Eyewear, Angel-style sunglasses, Springs collection, 2013 Designed by Ron Arad, a pioneer of 3D printing who trained as an architect at the Architectural Association (AA) in London, the glasses are printed using selective laser sintering (SLS) as a one-piece, one-material monolithic design with flexible joints that obviate the need for hinges.

RETHINKING ARCHITECTURE

Is it time, then, to reassess the nature of the profession of architecture? Now that 3D-printed body architecture and other digital design opportunities have opened up for architects, should we be rethinking the education and training of architects? For what has become clear is that the very skills that architects receive from their training are highly marketable in other arenas. What is equally clear is that the profession is struggling to survive in a period of volatile economic conditions, especially as the territory of the architect has been encroached on by other professionals within the construction industry, such as project managers, construction managers, engineers and quantity surveyors. Rather than trying to recover that lost territory, should architects not be trying to colonise other territories, such as 3D printing?

Could it be, then, that the evidence in this issue of ᗄ regarding the potential of 3D printing is sufficient to persuade those in charge to rethink the career pathways implicit in architectural education, so as to include other options beyond the construction industry? What would it be, for instance, to decouple architectural education from the accreditation process – often governed by somewhat parochial competition in a profession that has become global – and open it up to a more plural outlook, to include 3D-printed body architecture and other design fields?[10] As Antonelli notes (p 31), this would be in keeping with the tradition of the Bauhaus, where architecture was not differentiated from other forms of artistic expression. Indeed, the signs are already there. In some schools stronger students are now opting for 'Architectural Studies', a non-accredited option where they are free from the constraints of an accredited course and can customise their own education.

Such questions, however, lie beyond the scope of this publication. What is presented here is an account of an emerging commercially viable forum for architects to express their design abilities that is based on the field of 3D-printing technologies, and is opening up unexpected career opportunities. Above all, it is a new arena of architectural creativity operating at the scale of the human body – 3D-printed body architecture. ᗄ

Notes
1. The term 'body architecture' has been used by Lucy McRae to describe the use of her body in her design work: www.lucymcrae.net.
2. 'Florida International University Partners with MakerBot to Open 3D Printing Lab', *Prototype Today*, 2015: www.prototypetoday.com/tag/carta-innovation-lab.
3. Amy Frearson, 'Foster + Partners Works on "World's First Commercial Concrete-Printing Robot"', *Dezeen*, 25 November 2014: www.dezeen.com/2014/11/25/foster-partners-skanska-worlds-first-commercial-concrete-3d-printing-robot/; 'Foster + Partners Looking at Novel Approaches Towards Metal-Based 3D Printing as Part of LASIMM Consortium', Foster + Partners, 3 April 2017: www.fosterandpartners.com/news/archive/2017/04/foster-plus-partners-looking-at-novel-approaches-towards-metal-based-3d-printing-as-part-of-lasimm-consortium/; Neil Leach, '3D Printing in Space', in ᗄ *Space Architecture: The New Frontier for Design Research*, November/December (no 6), 2014, pp 108–13.
4. 'IAAC Revolutionizes the Construction Site at the Barcelona Building Construmat', Institute for Advanced Architecture of Catalonia (IAAC), 29 May 2017: www.iaacblog.com/life/iaac-revolutionizes-the-construction-site-at-the-barcelona-building-construmat/.
5. Marcus Vitruvius Pollo, *On Architecture*, trans Frank Granger, Harvard University Press (Cambridge, MA), 1931.
6. Brooke Hodge, Patricia Mears and Susan Sidlauskas, *Skin + Bones: Parallel Practices in Fashion and Architecture*, Thames & Hudson (London), 2006.
7. See Constance Adams, 'Alpha: From the International Style to the International Space Station', in ᗄ *Space Architecture*, op cit, pp 70–7.
8. Joseph Kosinski (director), *Tron: Legacy*, distributed by Walt Disney Pictures, 2010; Joseph Kosinski (director), *Oblivion*, distributed by Universal Pictures, 2013.
9. Mark Burry, 'The Aesthetics of Calculus (Roundtable Discussion)', in Neil Leach, David Turnbull and Chris Williams (eds), *Digital Tectonics*, John Wiley & Sons (London), 2004, p 145.
10. See Neil Leach, 'The (Ac)credit(ation) Card', in Peggy Deamer (ed), *The Architect as Worker: Immaterial Labor, the Creative Class, and the Politics of Design*, Bloomsbury (London), 2015, pp 228–40.

DERMIS

Neri Oxman and members of the Mediated Matter
Group in collaboration with Stratasys, *Vespers*,
Series 2, Mask 1,
'The New Ancient' collection,
Design Museum,
London,
2016

A GROWN WARDROBE FOR

Neri Oxman

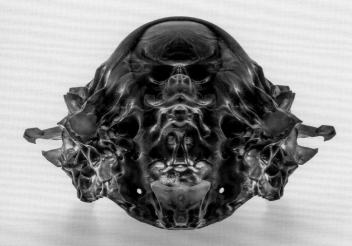

Using spatial mapping algorithms, culturally coded surface colorations and truncated geometries in the first series of the collection are transformed into coloured, internal strands within transparent, smoothly curved volumes in the second. The inner structures are entirely data driven, and designed to match the resolution of structures found in nature.

BODIES AND BUILDINGS

Stitching and assembly are yesterday's methods of wearables manufacturing. 3D printing, growing, and inbuilt responsive functionality are its future. The Mediated Matter Group founded by architect, designer, inventor and professor **Neri Oxman** at the Massachusetts Institute of Technology's Media Lab is showing the way. Here she describes some of the group's recent ventures: from a filtering cape and skirt, to an artificial organ system that provides useful microbes to the wearer, to a mask designed to capture a person's dying breath.

We have a rich and complex relationship with the garments we wear and the buildings we inhabit. Rich because it is abundant with properties, characteristics and matrices by which to evaluate the structural, corporeal, environmental and spatial performance of such artefacts; and complex because it is self-similar in the sense that both wearables and buildings act – at once – as barriers and as filters. The metaphor of the 'wearable building', however, appears to be moving beyond its timeless, and perhaps too simplistic, representation into one that is timely and tangible, unembroidered.

FROM DERMIS TO DOMUS
Novel technologies are gradually enabling architectural and product design-and-construction at nature's scale. We can seamlessly vary the physical properties of materials at the resolution of a sperm cell, a blood cell or a nerve cell. Stiffness, colour, transparency, conductivity – even smell and taste – can be individually tuned for each 3D pixel within a physical object. The generation of wearables is therefore no longer limited to assemblages of discrete fabrics with homogeneous properties that are stitched together. Rather, like organs, garments can be computationally 'grown' and 3D printed to form materially heterogeneous and multi-functional vessels.[1]

Such technologies express the spirit of the age in design, embodied within the archetypes created by them. Some archetypes, such as building skins, automobiles, aeroplanes and prosthetic devices, have evolved to improve the relationship between object, body and environment. Among them, wearables – or 'body architectures' – have in recent years come to occupy a unique place in the land of the printed and the grown.[2]

Applications related to functionally graded products – or structures that are designed to vary their properties within a single object – are already coming into their own: prosthetic sockets and splints can be designed with variable elasticity, structural beams can be designed with variable densities.[3] The smaller the scale, however, the easier it becomes to control and materialise the automation of physical properties. Which is to say: when you design a wearable you are designing a very small building.

This article examines how a collection of state-of-the-art 3D-printed wearables by the Mediated Matter Group, and the tools to create them, relate to the implied hypothesis above: that artefacts which unite information architectures and manufacturing practices – operating in high spatial resolution – will enable us to print rather than stitch, and grow rather than assemble.

THE FRAMEWORK
Due to recent advancements in additive manufacturing, the scales of making, printing and building are approaching the already micro scales of scanning and mapping. Consider, for example, the ease with which one can transition from an MRI scan of a residual limb to a 3D print of a prosthetic device. Or consider the ability to 3D-print synthetic, wearable skins designed to generate energy, sequester carbon or filter substances in and out of the body. Such synthetic, multi-material and bio-containing garments could operate like the human skin, as both barrier and filter. But they could also emulate, respond to, and even augment additional systems in the human corpus, bringing fashion – closer than it currently is – to the body.

The 'wearable constructions' illustrated here are ordered relative to a body system, which they are designed to emulate, amplify, augment, or 'reinterpret'. Systems include the integumentary system (skin: protection and filtration), the skeletal/muscular system (bones

and muscles: movement), the digestive system (gastrointestinal tract: energy creation) and the respiratory system (heart and lungs: breath). This systems-based approach, while not wholly rigorous, proposes a reading of the works as a collection pointing towards design opportunities that lie, dare we prophet, beneath the skin.

ANTHOZOA: THE INTEGUMENTARY SYSTEM
Anthozoa is a first of its kind 3D-printed apparel made of flexible and rigid materials. A cape and skirt modelled after the human skin (the integumentary system), the garment was 3D printed to act, at once, as a filtering barrier. The design combines a variety of materials and material properties, most notably rigidity and flexibility, within a single 'build'. Softer and more flexible materials were placed around the waist, while harder, more rigid materials were placed at the contours. The variation in elastic moduli, while worn on the body, contributed to the texture and movement of the garment.

Both shape and material composition of each structural component in the design are computationally defined to enable overall synergy between ergonomic fit, structural integrity, air (and sweat) filtration, as well as expression in motion. No two structural components are alike, and the original garment was designed without stitches. In this sense, the project challenges age-old couture traditions and offers a digital alternative by replacing needlework with code.

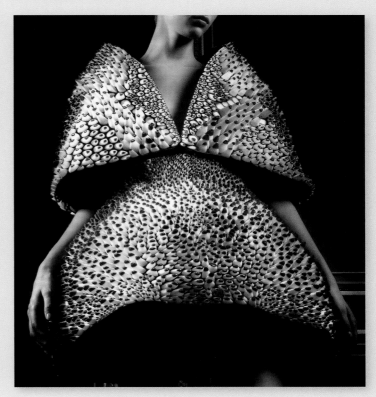

Neri Oxman and members of the Mediated Matter Group in collaboration with Stratasys and Iris van Herpen,
Anthozoa,
Museum of Fine Arts,
Boston,
Massachusetts,
2013

A collaboration with Professor W Craig Carter and Stratasys, the apparel was originally designed and constructed as a single 3D print without seams or stitches, combining flexible materials with tunable compliance.

Neri Oxman and
members of the
Mediated Matter Group
in collaboration with
Stratasys,
Rottlace,
2016

Series of masks designed for
Icelandic singer Björk. Left:
Material parameterisation
including distance fields
is generated and used to
assign material data to
each fibre. Right: Based
on parameterisation data,
properties are assigned that
enable gradual variation in
flexibility and translucency.

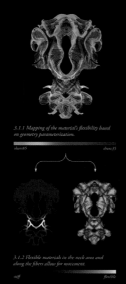

*3.1.1 Mapping of the material's flexibility based
on geometry parameterization.*

shore85 — *shore35*

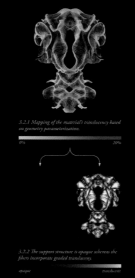

*3.2.1 Mapping of the material's translucency based
on geometry parameterization.*

0% — *20%*

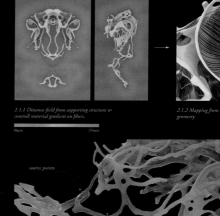

*2.1.1 Distance-field from supporting structure to
controll material gradient on fibers.*

0mm — *35mm*

*2.1.2 Mapping from distance-field to fiber
geometry.*

*3.1.2 Flexible materials in the neck area and
along the fibers allow for movement.*

stiff — *flexible*

*3.2.2 The support structure is opaque whereas the
fibers incorporate graded translucency.*

opaque — *translucent*

source points

*2.2.1 Geodesic distance-field within support structure to controll
rigidility and flexibility.*

0mm — *380mm*

Visualisations of the mask sub-
collection. Each mask comprises
over 20,000 individual fibres with
varying material properties in
stiffness and translucency.

ROTTLACE: THE SKELETAL/MUSCULAR SYSTEM

Rottlace is a family of masks designed for Icelandic singer-songwriter Björk. Inspired by her 2015 album *Vulnicura*, the Mediated Matter Group explored themes associated with self-healing and expressing 'the face without a skin'. The series originates with a mask that emulates Björk's facial structure and concludes with one that reveals a new identity, independent of its origin. What originates as a form of portraiture culminates in reincarnation.

The designs are informed by the geometrical and material logics that underlie the human musculoskeletal system; specifically, the complex structure of muscles, connective tissues, tendons and ligaments that modulate the human voice. This continuous weave of dense collagen fibres form functional 'typologies' of connections: muscle-to-bone, bone-to-bone and muscle-to-muscle.

As in the skeletal and muscular systems of the human body, where continuous, collagenous elements alter their chemical and mechanical properties as a function of the tension they exert or endure, each mask is designed as a synthetic 'whole without parts'. The masks incorporate tunable physical properties recapitulating, augmenting or controlling the facial form and movement behind them. Inspired by their biological counterpart, and conceived as 'muscle textile', the masks are bundled, multi-material structures, providing formal and structural integrity, as well as movement, to the face and neck.

The intricate fibrous tissue is made of soft and flexible materials designed to accommodate facial movement. The durometer of the materials varies as a function of the structural type they are intended to provide. Continuous property transitions – ranging from stiff bone-like structures, to semi-flexible ligament-like structures, to flexible fibre-based connective tissue structures – are computationally generated and digitally fabricated. Specifically, the fibrous tissue is computationally generated as modified principal curvature directions of Björk's facial scan, obtained as point cloud data, while the bone-like tissue emerges as support structure at points of high divergence from the principal curvature field. While bone-like locations are geometrically informed, their material composition is continuously graded, from stiff to flexible, and from opaque to transparent, as a function of geodesic distances given by the face scan.

Properties such as structure to material composition of the 3D-printed mask include a number of length scales, informing their mechanical properties and behaviour: (1) at the centimetre scale, the 3D-printed musculoskeletal system is designed to allow for flexible movement, while providing integrity to, and support of, its overall form; (2) at the millimetre scale, the fusing and parting of fibres with varying material compositions enables the overall structure to be self-supporting; and (3) at the micron scale, material droplets are placed, diffused and spatially aggregated to provide continuous material variation within a single 'muscle-skin' object.

The intricate fibrous tissue is made of soft and flexible materials designed to accommodate facial movement

Work in progress for the design of the final mask, including the subject's facial model. The 3D-printed tissue was computationally generated based on curvature directions of Björk's facial scan, obtained as point-cloud data.

Neri Oxman and
members of
the Mediated
Matter Group in
collaboration with
Stratasys,
Mushtari,
Cooper Hewitt,
Smithsonian
Design Museum,
New York,
2015

right: Visualisation of 100 iterative steps derived from three unique growth variations used to generate the fluidic wearable.

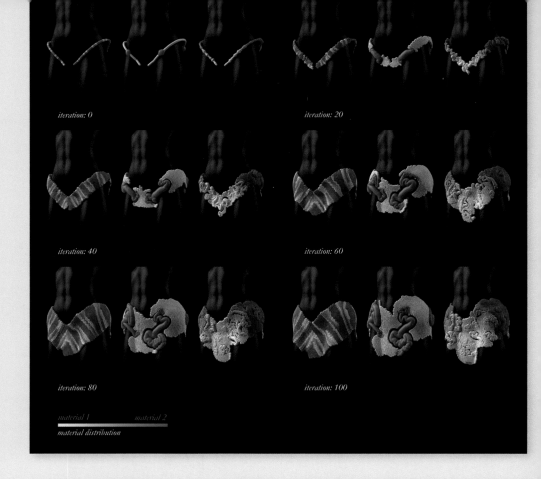

iteration: 0

iteration: 20

iteration: 40

iteration: 60

iteration: 80

iteration: 100

material 1   *material 2*

material distribution

(a) Effect of material transparency on microbial activity; (b) Implementation of a heterogeneous modelling approach; (c) Visualisation of the unfolded strand illustrating how the overall ('global') source-based approach influences local changes in opacity along the strand.

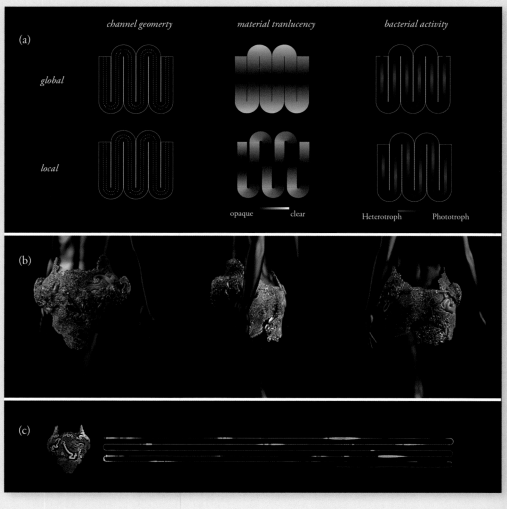

(a)

channel geomerty   *material tranlucency*   *bacterial activity*

global

local

opaque   clear   Heterotroph   Phototroph

(b)

(c)

Mushtari was designed to enable and inform a symbiotic relationship between two microorganisms

The *Mushtari* 3D-printed wearable combines a continuous internal network of biocompatible fluidic channels with variable optical transparency through the use of bitmap-based multi-material additive manufacturing.

MUSHTARI: THE DIGESTIVE SYSTEM

Buildings and bodies are not merely skin and bones. Both contain organ systems – manmade or biological – designed to sustain, maintain, enhance or attain equilibrium over space and time. Designing 'under the skin' requires a shift from top-down modelling approaches to bottom-up growth, both computational and biological.

Mushtari is a multi-material 3D-printed fluidic wearable designed to culture microbial communities for the purpose of energy generation. An artificial organ of sorts, it is designed after the gastrointestinal tract to convert solar energy into edible sugar. Think 'wearable micro-biome' or 'manmade digestive tract'. The wearable concept-piece was designed to function as a 'microbial factory', 58 metres (190 feet) long, which uses genetically modified microbes to make useful products for the wearer.

While 3D printing has been previously demonstrated as a viable means for the production of bespoke wearable-scale products, this technology has not previously been used to print a wearable with an inner fluidic network. Until recently, additive manufacturing has been utilised to produce microfluidic devices, but only in a single material and/or at a small scale (usually below feature sizes of 10 centimetres/4 inches) when compared to the scale of a typical wearable. *Mushtari* is the first-of-its-kind fluidic device with channels as thin as 1 millimetre (0.04 inches) in diameter. It was digitally fabricated at a wearable scale and examines the material ecology within a 3D-printed wearable that incorporates functional microbial communities.[4]

Mushtari was designed to enable and inform a symbiotic relationship between two microorganisms. Photosynthetic microbes could convert sunlight into nutrients for the heterotrophs, which could in turn produce compounds for specific applications. This form of microbial symbiosis, a phenomenon commonly found in nature, builds upon the inherent symbiosis present between the wearer and the microbes within the wearable. Based on the demonstrated biocompatibility for microbes shown in cytotoxicity tests of the 3D-printed materials used in the design, we can ultimately envision a fully functional photosynthetic prototype that contains engineered heterotrophs such that the wearer would be able to trigger microbial production of specific compounds of interest, including scents, pigments and fuels.[5]

The project demonstrates how controlled variation of geometric and optical properties at high spatial resolution – designed to facilitate biological functions – can be achieved through a combination of computational growth modelling and multi-material bitmap printing. This 'apparel fluidics' points towards design possibilities that lie at the intersection of computational design, additive manufacturing and synthetic biology, with the ultimate goal of imparting biological functionality to 3D-printed products.

LAZARUS AND *VESPERS*: THE RESPIRATORY SYSTEM

They say that in every breath of fresh air we take, there are molecules exhaled by Jesus, Cleopatra and Julius Caesar in their dying breath. In a very physical way, we live among the spirits, and they live among us. *Lazarus* is a mask designed to contain the wearer's last breath. It is the precursor – a kernel – for a larger collection of masks, entitled *Vespers*, that speculate on and offer a new interpretation of the ancient death mask.[6]

Traditionally made of a single material, such as wax or plaster, the death mask originated as a means of capturing a person's visage, keeping the deceased 'alive' through memory. *Lazarus* serves as an

Neri Oxman and members of
the Mediated Matter Group
in collaboration with
Stratasys,
Lazarus,
Design Museum,
London,
2016

opposite: Using a functional
advection workflow, the resulting
3D-printed mask (printed from
rigid white and transparent
materials) is shown alongside its
corresponding 3D rendering.

Visualisation of the design approach.
In (a), (b) and (c), data sources are
generated. In (d) the data sources are
transferred to the object of interest,
which is detailed in (e), (f) and (g).

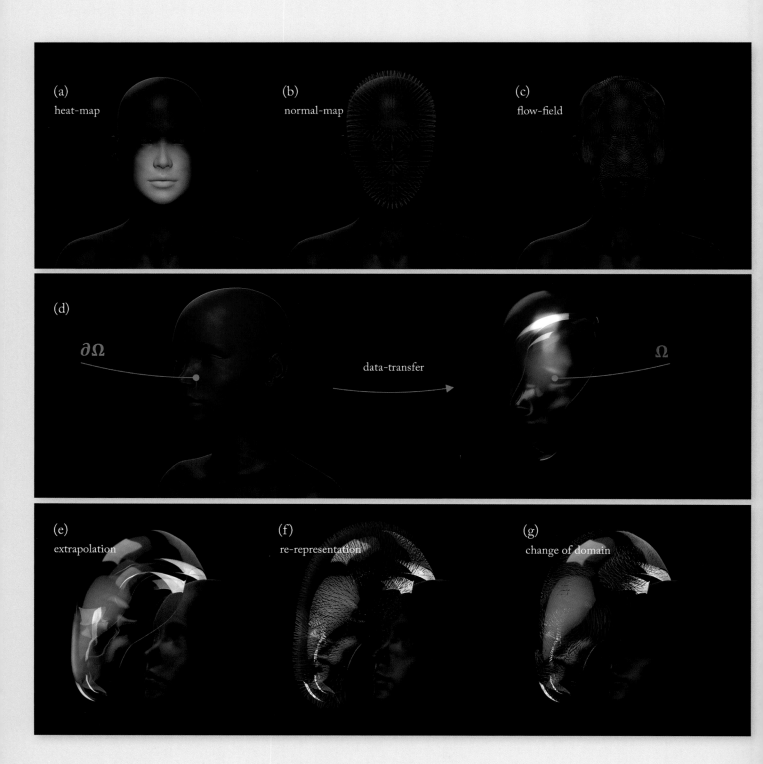

(a) heat-map

(b) normal-map

(c) flow-field

(d) $\partial\Omega$ data-transfer Ω

(e) extrapolation

(f) re-representation

(g) change of domain

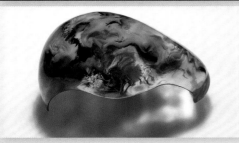

'air urn' memento that is a new form of 3D-printed portraiture, combining the wearer's facial features while serving as a spatial enclosure for their last breath. The mask's surface is modelled after the face of the dying person, and its material composition is informed by the physical flow of air and its distribution across the surface. Unlike its traditional hand-made analogue, the design of *Lazarus* is entirely data driven, digitally generated and additively manufactured. It approaches the resolution of the physical phenomenon that it is designed to capture, thereby creating a unique artefact that is perfectly customised to fit the wearer and her last breath.[7]

The design and production of *Lazarus* embodies a data-driven approach for the creation of high-resolution, geometrically complex and materially heterogeneous 3D-printed objects at product scale. Entitled 'data-driven material modelling' (DdMM), this approach utilises external and user-generated data sets for the modelling of heterogeneous material distributions during slice generation, thereby enabling the production of voxel-matrices describing material distributions for bitmap printing at the 3D printer's native voxel resolution. To enable this approach, the Mediated Matter Group has developed a bitmap-slicing framework designed to inform material property distribution in concert with slice generation.[8]

The *Vespers* collection comprises three series, each with five masks that are related through time. Modelled after *Lazarus*, the second series – the present – illustrated here explores the transition between life and death, illustrating the progression of the death mask from a symbolic cultural relic, as represented in the first series (the past), to a functional biological interface, as revealed in the third series (the future). It moves beyond the exterior surface and into the interior volume of the mask, employing a contemporaneous interpretation of the soul's journey.[9]

This second series elucidates embryonic forms through complex internal geometries as it prepares to support the re-engineered life of the third series. In this series, it is the interplay of light that reveals the internal structures. Like spirits (from the Latin '*spiritus*', meaning 'breath'), these structures reference the distribution of the martyr's last breath.[10]

FROM DOMUS TO DERMIS

In the near future, wearable constructions will be conceived as extensions of our bodies. Designed to embody functionality, and made of engineered living matter, 3D-printed living apparel will far surpass the performance of both single-material 'dumb fibres' and antiquated assemblies made of mono-material parts. But designing in nature's way is far from natural. It will require computational growth, additive manufacturing on cellular-length scales, microorganisms synthetically engineered to sustain life, a fibre-based bioreactor, and so much more. While I am confident we are well on our way, I still wonder: will dermis (nature) ever look up to domus (architecture)? I shall live and grow for that day. ∆

Notes
1. Neri Oxman, 'Vespers: A Collection of Death Masks', *Fear and Love: Reactions to a Complex World*, exhibition catalogue, Design Museum (London), 2016.
2. *Ibid*.
3. Neri Oxman, 'Towards a Material Ecology', World Economic Forum, Davos, 2016: www.weforum.org/agenda/2016/01/towards-a-material-ecology/.
4. Christoph Bader *et al*, 'Grown, Printed and Biologically Augmented: An Additively Manufactured Microfluidic Wearable, Functionally Templated for Synthetic Microbes', *3D Printing and Additive Manufacturing*, 3 (2), 2016, pp 79–89.
5. *Ibid*.
6. Neri Oxman, 'Vespers', *op cit*.
7. *Ibid*.
8. Christoph Bader *et al*, *op cit*.
9. Neri Oxman, 'Vespers', *op cit*.
10. *Ibid*. Scientific research into biologically informed digital fabrication underlining this collection was supported in part by GETTY LAB.

Neil Leach

AN INTERVIEW
WITH MOMA'S
PAOLA ANTONELLI

CURATING THE DIGITAL

Janne Kyttanen,
Sofa So Good,
2014

The mesh design for
the sofa was inspired
by spiders' webs and
silkworm cocoons, and
uses just 2.5 litres (4
gallons) of resin for a
sofa 1.5 metres (5 feet)
in length.

As Senior Curator in the Department of Architecture and Design at the Museum of Modern Art, New York, **Paola Antonelli** treats digital and analogue design with equal regard. Here she talks to Guest-Editor **Neil Leach** about some of her decisions. She discusses the distinctions between design, art and architecture; how she keeps a clear head amid the prevailing euphoria over new technologies, in order to choose only those pieces that also represent successful design; whom she views as paragons of design in the digital age; and why she believes that architectural education needs to be reinvented.

Patrick Jouin,
One_shot.MGX Stool,
Museum of Modern
Art (MoMA),
New York,
2006

opposite: Selective laser sintering (SLS) was used to produce the entire seating surface, legs and hidden integral articulations of this stool in just one shot.

Patrick Jouin,
C2 Solid Chair,
Museum of Modern
Art (MoMA),
New York, 2004

The chair was manufactured using stereolithography, a 3D-printing process in which a computer-controlled laser heats and solidifies a photosensitive epoxy resin upon contact.

Paola Antonelli trained as an architect at the Polytechnic of Milan, and is currently Senior Curator of the Department of Architecture and Design as well as Director of R&D at the Museum of Modern Art (MoMA) in New York. An avid supporter of the digital realm, she has exhibited 3D-printed works by several of the contributors to this issue of Δ, and acquired some of them for the museum's permanent collection.

Antonelli is a great champion of design. She believes that design is the highest form of creative expression, and that it is everywhere: 'I want people to understand that design is so much more than cute chairs, that it is first and foremost everything around us in our life.'[1] Moreover, for her, design is not so much a discipline as 'a constructive attitude'.

Famously, Antonelli has claimed that design is not a form of art, and that art is not a form of design. At least in most cases. This is to say that artists do not necessarily make good designers, and she is sceptical of those who view art as a loftier discipline: 'The worst is when artists think they can just "descend" towards design, thinking that they have had a higher training, a higher calling, and they can thus scale it down, bring it down to the level of a design object.' By way of example she cites the furniture designed by the American minimalist artist Donald Judd, which she regards as expensive, uncomfortable, and even dangerous 'because it rips your stockings and gives you bruises'. By contrast, she is highly appreciative of the design work of the artist Martin Puryear, known for his use of traditional crafts: 'When asked whether he wanted to design an object to sell in the MoMA store on the occasion of his [2008] retrospective, he designed an amazing pan scraper, a tool to clean pots and pans, a thing that had nothing to do with his art, had nothing to do with his usual materials. All of a sudden this man of incredible talent took his talent and just put it, as if it were a beating heart, from an art body into a design body.'

Significantly, however, Antonelli does see architecture as a branch of design: 'Design can be applied to many different contexts and many different scales, and architecture is one of them.' At the same time, she acknowledges that this approach might not be universal: 'Not everybody feels comfortable with the idea of architecture being part of design, and not vice versa.' She developed this approach as a result of her experiences when curating the 'Design and the Elastic Mind' exhibition at MoMA in 2008: 'It was an exhibition about design and science, and it was divided into three areas that had to do with scale, which meant – at first we thought – with size. There was a micro- and nano-scale area, a human-scale area, and then a large-scale area. What we discovered was that scale was no longer a matter of size, but rather a matter of complexity. We discovered that dimensionality had taken on a completely different meaning. So even in the large-scale area we featured investigations of microscopic phenomena and also of phenomena that have no dimensions whatsoever – like a map of the Internet. It doesn't make sense any more to distinguish design disciplines because of the materials they use, the dimensional scale they tackle, or other old-school kinds of criteria.'

However, it is not always that easy for architects to shift in scale. Nor is it simply a question of just changing scale; of architects 'shrinking' their designs to the body scale, as in the title of the movie *Honey, I Shrunk the Kids* (1989).[2] As Antonelli says: 'There are designers who are able to work all scales seamlessly well, but not all of them. I consider architects as designers that work with buildings and other architectural applications. Sometimes they can jump scale and dimensions, and sometimes they can't. Not all scales work for all talents.'

MOMA AND THE DIGITAL DOMAIN

Antonelli also has an interest in the digital domain. One of her most controversial acts was to bring video games into the MoMA collection, starting in 2012. In 1995 she learnt to write HTML code in order to compose the website for her first MoMA show, 'Mutant Materials in Contemporary Design', which went on to become the museum's main website. Importantly, however, she does not distinguish between digital and analogue design. For her they are both design: 'I personally don't make a differentiation. The digital is one of the dimensions of life. I don't

The challenge was to try to marry the aesthetic concerns that lie at the heart of MoMA with the euphoria for the new technology

Janne Kyttanen,
Avoid Chandelier,
2016

3D-printed circular light
fitting with an intricate
diamond structure
finished in copper.

want to use the expression "digital life".' Moreover, as virtual reality begins to embrace haptics, that difference is further eroded: 'Right now, virtual reality is still very cumbersome and not seamless. One day we'll be able not only to make it be much more portable (hopefully we won't have to wear helmets), but also we will be able to use our sense of touch. So at that point if the digital dimension of our lives can also sustain haptics, what does it mean to talk about digital design? Why differentiate? Let's start thinking about it as just another dimension.'

At MoMA, this interest in the digital actually predates the arrival of Antonelli herself: 'Interestingly, the attention to the digital had begun at MoMA a long time ago. There was a great exhibition in the late 1990s called "Information Art" that was about the diagrams that electronic engineers used to check and make sure that microchips were designed correctly. They were magnifications of the microchips that were then plotted out, framed, and hung on the walls of the gallery. Cara McCarty was one of the curators at that time, and she showed that these diagrams could look almost like urban planning schemes – and like art.'

Antonelli started collecting 3D-printed objects for MoMA early on: 'It must have been around 2004 – or earlier – that we acquired our first 3D-printed objects from MGX, the 3D manufacturing company in Belgium.' However, the challenge was to try to marry the aesthetic concerns that lie at the heart of MoMA with the euphoria for the new technology, and what appears technologically advanced might not always work in design terms: 'For instance, do you remember Swedish design group Front's famous Sketch Furniture? Of course we showed it in "Design and the Elastic Mind" – it was amazing. And of course we marvelled at it. But we didn't put it in the collection because as design that really doesn't work. The designers meant it to be a demo. It's the technology that is really arresting. So it was only in the temporary exhibition.'

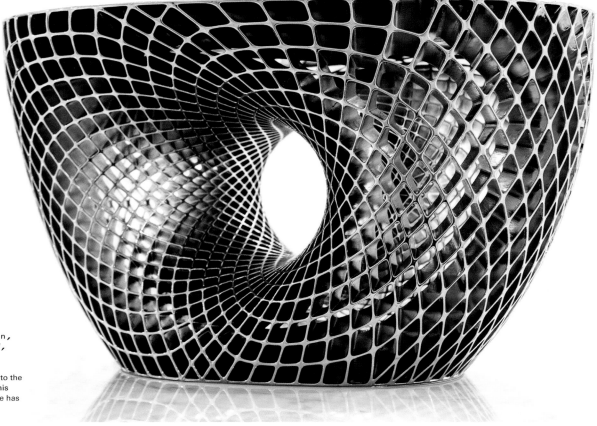

Janne Kyttanen,
Rhodium Avoid,
2016

A companion piece to the
Avoid Chandelier, this
3D-printed side table has
a rhodium finish.

Antonelli herself is somewhat cautious about the current euphoria for home-produced 3D printing: 'Every time there's a new technology – as you know very well – there is a moment of enthusiastic adoption, almost drunkenness, and so you see a lot of poor work pouring in. Then too much of it happens, enough becomes enough, people start becoming critical, and sobriety hits. Then you start seeing a certain maturity, not only technological, but also functional and aesthetic.' And yet even with this early work, there are occasional glimpses of the real potential of 3D printing: 'We started out with a piece by Finnish digital sculptor Janne Kyttanen, and then some of the first pieces we acquired were by French industrial designer Patrick Jouin. He had done the *C2 Solid Chair* [2004] and then the beautiful *One_shot.MGX Stool* [2006]. They are still in the collection. So they were early examples, but they were already quite elegant examples of what 3D printing could do.'

Yet for Antonelli 3D printing is still too expensive and unwieldy: 'It has promise, but for it to become really part of the world we need to all believe in it and invest in it to bring the prices down.' Nor indeed does everything need to be 3D printed: 'First of all, says who that everything should be 3D printed? Why should it be necessary to 3D-print cities? Sometimes it's good to also use manual labour. Sometimes humans do it better. Humans also need employment. Once again, it is about the "drunken moment".'

'I have always insisted on the fact that physical elegance… is a form of communication'

Janne Kyttanen,
4-in-1 Dress,
2014

Part of the artist's 'Lost Luggage' series, where files are sent to be printed at an eventual destination so that the traveller does not need to bring any luggage on the journey.

ARCHITECTURAL EDUCATION

She also thinks it important to reinvent architectural education in our digital age. In some senses we need to go back to the spirit of the Bauhaus, where architecture was not taught as a separate discipline, but was part of a broader design enquiry. But at the same time students need to be taught core principles: 'Everybody who studied at the Bauhaus went through a primary curriculum that was very much about learning the rudiments of all the arts, and then branching out. That kind of initial core is, in my opinion, still extremely important.'

Antonelli considers herself fortunate for having studied at the Polytechnic of Milan, where she was exposed to a lot of theory, history and science and very little practice, unfortunately, but where that theory went very deep: 'I was there at a moment of complete chaos because we were 15,000 students, only in architecture, and only in that school. I learnt about engineering, about construction science. I did maths, and I took all the scientific exams. There were some great teachers, and I had drawn my own curriculum. I believe that if you have a strong engineering, historical and theoretical background then you can move in any direction you want. There is risk in being completely fluid, "artistic" from the start. I think that the beginning of a design education needs to be rigorous and rigid. And then it can soften and open up.'

And who would be a perfect example of such an approach – one that marries technical knowledge and design ability? Antonelli cites Neri Oxman [see her article on pp 16–25 of this issue], whose work she first showed in 'Design and the Elastic Mind' in 2008: 'She has the aesthetic and crafts talent that is necessary to convey to a wide audience concepts that are scientifically complicated and that would not be otherwise understood. Formal elegance can be a powerful tool of communication. And still, nobody can say that Neri is just producing pretty things, because the science behind them is so solid that nobody can question their contribution to a deeper conversation. That's what I love about her work, that in all of her investigations she is crystal clear and assertive when it comes to the science, and still she leaves everyone with their mouth agape at the beauty of the objects that express those complex scientific constructs.'

Neri Oxman/
Mediated Matter Group,
Glass 3D printer,
MIT Media Lab,
Massachusetts Institute
of Technology (MIT),
Cambridge,
Massachusetts,
2015

The molten-glass material is
heated up to approximately
1,037˚C (1,900°F) in a kiln cartridge,
and then funnelled through an
alumina-zircon-silica nozzle.

Neri Oxman/
Mediated Matter Group,
Glass I,
MIT Media Lab,
2015

Above and opposite: The project synthesises modern technologies with age-old established glass tools and techniques to produce novel glass structures with numerous potential applications.

'It's almost like in nature, where the first means of communication is form'

THE QUESTION OF BEAUTY

Antonelli has very lucid views when she speaks of beauty: 'I have always insisted on the fact that physical elegance – when I say "physical elegance" I don't mean universal platonic beauty, I mean formal incisiveness within cultures and subcultures – is a form of communication. It's almost like in nature, where the first means of communication is form. The same happens with human beings; at first, we communicate with form. If you were able to take a complex scientific concept and manifest it so that its gorgeous appearance cuts across resistance and disbelief, then you're going to have a better chance to not only prove your scientific concept to your peers, but also to reach a wider audience.'

Here she refers to the example of the 3D-printed glasswork Neri Oxman produced within the framework of her Mediated Matter Group at the MIT Media Lab: 'Explaining some of the concepts of viscosity and how the slurp of molten glass deposits one layer over the other scientifically is one thing. By showing it so elegantly – not only in its final form, but also in the video, building a molten-glass 3D printer and showing the process – that is a precious service to science because it is able to bring along an audience of non-scientists who will be mesmerised by the beauty and the high production quality of the science/design/art-work.'

Antonelli is highly impressed not only by the work that Oxman produces, but also by the way in which she talks about her work: 'I think Neri should be taken as a paragon not only of science, but also of how to bring science into the world and talk about it. It's also a matter of stringing the world along. When you're an innovator and when you have groundbreaking ideas you need to find a way to let the world know about them.' ⌂

This article is based on a telephone conversation between Neil Leach and Paola Antonelli in January 2017.

Notes
1. Paola Antonelli, 'Why I brought Pac-Man to MoMA', TED Talk, TED Salon, New York, 2013: www.ted.com/talks/paola_antonelli_why_i_brought_pacman_to_moma/transcript.
2. Joe Johnson (director), *Honey, I Shrunk the Kids*, distributed by Walt Disney Pictures, 1989.

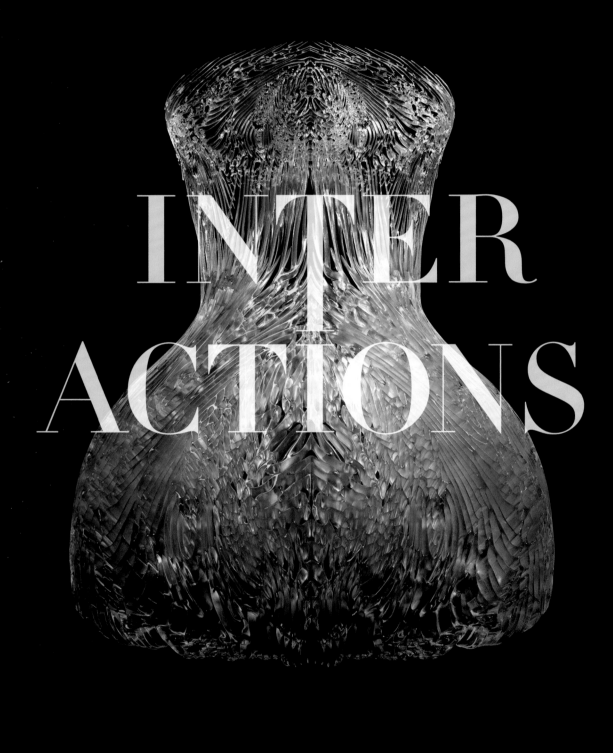

DIALOGUES ON BODY, PROTECTIONS AND DERIVATIVES

INTER ACTIONS

Niccolò Casas and Iris van Herpen,
Magnetic Motion dress,
Iris van Herpen 'Magnetic Motion'collection,
2015 Spring/Summer Ready-to-Wear Paris
Fashion Week,
Paris,
September 2014

The Magnetic Motion dress, the first collaboration between architect Niccolò Casas and fashion designer Iris van Herpen, derives from the idea that fashion and architecture can overlap if interpreted in terms of relations: between space and body, between bodies and bodies, and between objects and body.

Could kinetic clothing be the next big thing? A collaboration between Dutch fashion designer Iris van Herpen and Italy-based architect and educator **Niccolò Casas** has produced a series of dresses that blur the boundaries between the body and the space around it. Casas explains how they have fused handcraft with technology, using 3D printing, mass customisation techniques, and morpho-dynamic simulations, among other means, to produce couture pieces that react to bodily movement in extraordinary new ways.

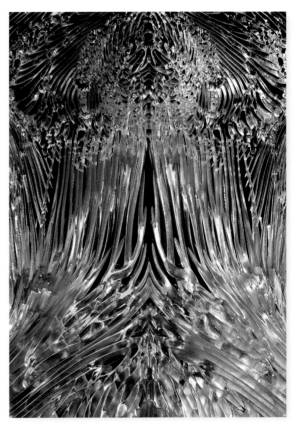

Detail. The Magnetic Motion dress acts as a semi-rigid shell protecting the body: the dress, the body and the space around the body are never completely integrated, thus maintaining a certain autonomy. This tension between action and reaction intensifies all three.

Thanks to the possibilities of dialogues afforded by new communicative technologies, new hybrid disciplines and collaborative exchanges are now emerging across both artistic and scientific fields. The fertility of these dialogues is such that professionals in various different disciplines can exchange ideas and open up possibilities for new applications of their work. As a consequence, the role of the architect has changed tremendously, with architecture being seen not only in the form of built space but also as a space of interactions. An architect is a designer of relational systems, both physical and immaterial, and is thus becoming a new professional figure that cuts across disciplines and scales with a focus on aesthetics, performance, society and innovation.

At the same time, the fashion industry is currently experiencing the digital revolution that architecture went through in the 1990s, with parametric design and production processes deriving from architecture, computer graphics and engineering. Scripting and algorithmic tools, together with advanced fabrication technologies, are making new performative aesthetics possible. Apparel is therefore no longer limited to the fashion audience, but is becoming a territory of interface and experimentation: additive manufacturing and so-called 'future materials' can enhance on-demand production and promote recycling and waste reduction, while synthetic biology and bio-fabrication can make fashion more sustainable and less harmful.

There exists a sort of continuous process of design investigation in which the body, its movements and interactions act as a 'centre of gravity'; from this perspective, technologies force designers to think in terms of relations: between space and body, between bodies and bodies, and between objects and body. The boundaries of the living (interacting) human being, its protection (clothing, building and infrastructure) and derivatives (information, culture, media and, finally, art) are being challenged by these new interdisciplinary conversations.

It is in this context that my collaboration with Iris van Herpen started. Van Herpen is a Dutch fashion designer who continuously pushes the boundaries of fashion design, inventing new forms and methods of sartorial expression. She achieves this by combining the most traditional and the most radical materials and garment construction methods into her unique aesthetic vision. She calls this design ethos 'New Couture'.

The collaboration was grounded in a shared interest in the tension and the synergy between the three-dimensionality of the body and the three-dimensionality 'around the body': space,

dress and person are integrated but are still independent systems, each of which intensifies and amplifies the others.

Searching for newness, our research focused on the possibilities offered by the application of additive manufacturing and digital design to couture, and together we teamed up on two art pieces and five dresses. Our collaborative research followed three specific phases: exploration, articulation and integration. The first step was the formal investigation (the exploration of novel aesthetic qualities offered by additive technologies and 3D design software). The second was the inclusion of functional properties (the dynamic features), and the third focused on the combination of digital and traditional craftsmanship. Each step came as an evolution and, therefore, as an incorporation and extension of the previous one.

EXPLORATION

Our first collaboration was the Magnetic Motion dress, created for the Iris van Herpen 'Magnetic Motion' collection, shown in September 2014 at the 2015 Spring/Summer Ready-to-Wear Paris Fashion Week. The dress design resulted from experiments on magnetic fields and ferrofluids conducted with the artist Jólan van der Wiel that I extended through digital simulations and design. By examining the representation of dynamic forces of attraction and repulsion, our goal was to erase the boundaries between nature and technology.

The project explored the idea of solidified motion using the luminescent glow of clear-cut forms offered by the newly introduced 3D-printable material Accura® ClearVue™ by 3D Systems. This stereolithography (SLA) material was selected because of its ability to create a high level of detail, delicate refinement and translucent quality. The intricacy of the design is perfectly matched with the elegance of the material, which encourages a play of light and shadow; the dress emanates a dainty sensation of fragility, with crystallised flows giving it an appearance of ice – effects that would have been impossible with traditional design techniques and materials.

The (digitally controlled) structure of the cloth was offset by the chaotic and natural pattern inspired by the nature of magnetic growth; no two printed elements are alike. Manufactured as a combined front and back, the first panel took 45 hours, and the second 36. This process was then followed by nearly eight hours of polishing and finishing: digital and traditional craftsmanship working together. The dress was a challenge to create in the short timeframe available, and also quite a feat of engineering: the technicians' initial response to the idea was

Niccolò Casas and Iris van Herpen, Hacking Infinity dress, Iris van Herpen 'Hacking Infinity' collection, 2015-16 Fall/Winter Ready-to-Wear Paris Fashion Week, Paris, March 2015

The Hacking Infinity dress marks a radical change from the earlier 3D-printed rigid dresses. In order to infer dynamic properties, the dress is broken down into 6,556 independent but interconnected components, all of which are different.

The design and construction of the Hacking Infinity dress are largely driven by the nature of the material; its appearance, strength and resistance guided, via scripting solutions, the size, the direction and the distribution of the spikes.

'99.99 per cent, it's going to fail', yet they tried and succeeded! Additionally, the strapless, semitranslucent minidress was designed specifically for Dutch model Iekeliene Stange, and 3D printed in structural pieces that were custom fitted to her slender form. After finalising the dress's 3D design, a scan of the dressmaker's form was made to match the model's body for the final file to print. Again, this was a new form of design interaction made possible by digital technologies.

ARTICULATION

The Magnetic Motion dress represents the ultimate point in a certain direction. The boundaries of the collaboration were pushed further for the following piece: the Hacking Infinity dress, made for the Iris van Herpen 'Hacking Infinity' collection and exhibited in March 2015 at the 2015–16 Fall/Winter Ready-to-Wear Paris Fashion Week.

In the search for kinetic properties, the new dress loses continuity, thus becoming fragmented. This was made possible by developing a knitting system that engendered motion and overcame the idea of crystallised movement, representing a radical departure from Van Herpen's earlier sculptural pieces. Comprised of four panels of interconnected parts, the dress has miniature teeth that interlock and act as a dynamic community. In this way, the SLA dress combines motion and complexity: it acts as an ecosystem of unique individual components that continuously react to the body's movement.

This result was only possible thanks to 3D-printing technology and the opportunity to mass-customise unique pieces: all 6,556 components are different. The variation was driven both by the body's interaction (so as to facilitate movement) and the aesthetic sensibility. The four panels were 3D printed in the transparent Accura ClearVue material by 3D Systems; their team in Tennessee took care to optimise the 3D file, then followed this with nearly 200 cumulative hours of printing production and two hours of delicate manual support removal. The dress was an astounding undertaking, both for fashion and technology: the small spikes of the SLA dress are one of the most extreme articulations of how materials can evolve and silhouettes can dynamically change.

Comprised of four panels of interconnected parts, the dress has miniature teeth that interlock and act as a dynamic community

INTEGRATION

Our latest collaboration – for the 2016 Iris van Herpen 'Lucid' collection, shown at the 2015–16 Fall/Winter Haute Couture Paris Fashion Week in March 2015 – required the sum of all our collaborative experiences. In the search for dynamic properties combined with aesthetic complexity and structural variation, technology was fused with handcraft. The collection featured two 3D-printed Magma dresses that combined a flexible TPU material, creating a fine web, together with polyamide rigid printing. This time we joined forces with the Belgium-based 3D company Materialise. The Magma dresses represent a further step on from the Magnetic Motion dress. The Magma dresses are not only a dynamic combination of 3D-printed rigid components, but a system that merges 3D-printed flexible and rigid materials with traditional craftsmanship. Its components are no longer interwoven but, through a simple 'hidden design system', kept together by the TPU net in combination with a specific knitting technique. This new combination allows for unprecedented capabilities of flexibility and adaptability without the problems of stretching.

One of the dresses was stitched from 6,052 3D-printed elements. All the components are unique; they differentiate – changing in shape and direction – depending on the body's position, so as to adapt and amplify according to the model's movement. The other dress, on the contrary, loses its rigid elements, so as to evidence a light and delicate 3D-printed flexible lace that gently shapes itself to the body's curvatures.

With time, new design techniques and algorithms were created in order to include both the nature of the materials and the gestures of the body; the results were not limited to new aesthetic performances, but also to a new elegant system comprising the body, garment and space.

One of the Magma dresses loses its rigid components, revealing its light flexible 3D-printed lace. Freed from its technical reason of being (to provide support and stretch), the pattern acquires a new aesthetic dimension.

The Magma dresses are a system that merges 3D-printed flexible and rigid materials with traditional craftsmanship.

REDEFINITION

The transformation and evolvement of the 3D-printed dress seem linear and coherent, but in a similar way to natural processes, in practice, this emerged from a large number of attempts and dead-ends. Over the years, a series of multi-material combinations and a series of different pattern and component designs were developed and evaluated: some tests simply did not work well enough, while others were too immature for the technologies available at the time. Errors and failures, often seen as mistakes, are in reality an essential part of design evolution: every process is filled with faults and frictions, but it is essentially in the overcoming of them that improvement and optimisation arise. Every new invention is temporary and it lays the foundation for its further advancement.

Nevertheless, innovation is superimposed on (interlaced with) the existing. The new does not (always) eliminate the old; rather, it comes as an integration. While significantly pushing the limits of 3D-printing machines it becomes clear that traditional manufacturing techniques can provide the answers to the problems of digital ones. At the same time, traditional procedures can be completely redefined through their integration with new ones, thus leading to unexpected retroactive effects. In a way, the future and the past constantly interact (act and react to each other) in a continuous moment of creation which is the present. ᴆ

top: The Magma dresses resulted from the redefinition of traditional couture-stitching techniques, via their interaction with computer-driven manufacturing procedures: the moment you change the way you design, you also change the way you think about design.

middle: Similar patterns tend to emerge at different scales in different domains. The Magma dresses' organic look naturally derives from the nature of the materials, the components' structure, and the relation with the moving body: a dynamic infrastructure arising on a bodyscape.

bottom: The 21 panels that form the flexible 3D-printed lace gently interact with the cloth underneath, allowing the Magma dress to move and bend in an unexpected and peculiar way. This differs from traditional dresses and also from wholly 3D-printed dresses, precisely because of this novel combination.

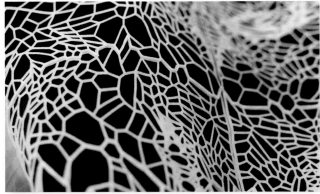

DIGIT
CRAF
COUT

Julia Koerner in collaboration with Iris van Herpen,
Biopiracy dress, 2014-15 Fall/Winter Ready-to-Wear Paris Fashion Week,
March 2014

Organic petals are nested intricately around the figure of the human body.
This garment was printed by Materialise in Belgium, utilising laser sintering technology and flexible material.

Julia Koerner in collaboration with Iris van Herpen,
Hybrid Holism dress, 2012-13 Fall/Winter Haute-Couture Paris Fashion Week,
July 2012

The digitally crafted stark contrast between underlying parametrically pleated surfaces and organically modelled
leaves creates intricate three-dimensional spaces, reminiscent of the human body.

Julia Koerner,
Venus dress,
'Porifera' collection,
Spring Studios,
London,
June 2016

The tessellated, net-like weave
is based on a point cloud and
adapts to the characteristics
and proportions of the wearer.

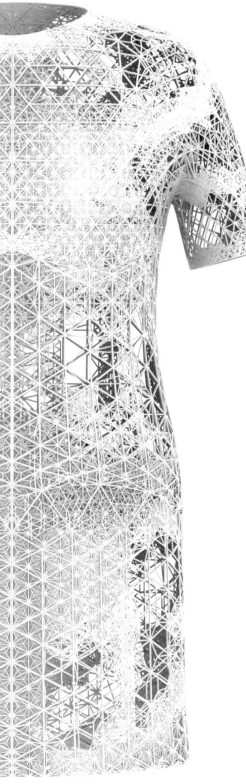

Clothing could be described as architecture in motion. **Julia Koerner**, a designer based between Salzburg and Los Angeles, operates at the crossroads between architecture and product design. She has recently been working on a number of projects in the couture field, both independently and in collaboration. Here she describes how these creations – largely inspired by the forms and growth patterns of nature – have utilised various additive manufacturing techniques to explore the possibilities of folding, nesting and smocking in digital space. From seamlessness to the ability to adapt to temperature, light and emotion, these garments appear to naturally grow on the body or to animate it.

Generative design processes have unravelled a new dimension. Architects are bridging scales and crossing disciplines between architecture and fashion. Coco Chanel once said, 'Fashion is architecture: it is a matter of proportions.'[1] Technological advancements in manufacturing, specifically 3D printing, have unveiled a potential to manifest complex digitally generated forms into physical and tangible objects. Digital design processes vary based on scale and tolerances. Of specific relevance today is computational design at the convergence of emergent technologies and material performance within the fashion industry. Architects typically design static structures which do not move with their occupants. In fashion, garments are all about flexibility and movement. Trained as an architect, the fashion designer Pierre Balmain has expressed that 'dressmaking is the architecture of movement, nothing is more important in a dress than its construction.'[2]

In biology there is no distinction between materiality and structure.[3] 3D printing resembles how structures grow in nature. The process relies on the bonding of material between different layers. Hierarchies in geometry allow for a structural behaviour reminiscent of natural systems. Nature provides us with intelligent, dynamic and optimised evolutionary forms. These forms are also beautiful. Designing an object in motion seeks an elegance and aesthetic found in the DNA of organic and natural forms. The synthesis of nature and technology often involves digital analysis and research into the mathematical logic and properties of artefacts found in the biodiversity of nature. Two-dimensional surface relief and crusts of organic mass in combination with the three-dimensional complexity of cellular systems can serve as guiding principles for structural performance and intricate geometry. The architectural micro scale of deep-sea sponges, kelp, hymenium, spores and corals are a design resource for the morphology of garments. 3D scanning, computed tomography (CT) and macro imagery are used to capture and analyse natural structures. An intriguing aspect of this form of research is the embodiment of a beautiful organic aesthetic. The combination of mathematics, engineering and computational design with an aesthetic design sensibility result in a re-creation of this beautiful organic quality, in a highly discretised process.

The interplay between fashion and architecture is illustrated in a series of digitally crafted and 3D-printed garment designs described below.

SEAMS AND PART-TO-WHOLE RELATIONSHIP

The seamless translation of a continuous form out of the machine is an incredible advancement in digital fabrication. In fashion, 3D digital garment design eliminates the need for seam locations for cutting patterns and blueprints. They are irrelevant now. The additive manufacturing process determines new locations of seams in relation to the size and bounding box of the machine build platform. Further, the locations of seams depend on the decision of the computational designer who develops strategies of assembly from part to whole. Although printing full scale is possible with some technologies, most 3D-printed garments are still printed in parts. The part-to-whole relationship between individual 3D-printed elements is important to consider when designing digitally constructed pieces. In some instances the seams are purposefully hidden within the layering construct of the volumetric designs. Other times strategies are developed to reveal individually printed elements. Architects specialised in material connections between multiple parts can leverage this three-dimensional understanding to develop a seamless design.

WEAVE, STRUCTURE AND ADAPTATION

The research for the 2016 3D-printed Venus dress was based on analysis of the deep-sea sponge, also known as Venus' flower basket. The woven net-like structure grows based on environmental influences and adapts to its surroundings. It is influenced by light and water currents. The 3D-printed dress is a woven and tessellated matrix generated from a point cloud. This is mapped based on characteristics and dimensions of the wearer. The dress also reacts to the wearer by using heat-mapping technology to highlight their emotions. Some parts of the dress are 3D printed using biodegradable polylactic acid (PLA) filament, adapting to temperature and touch. It also changes colour according to its environment.

For this 3D-printed dress a digital algorithm develops a triangulated structural weave, inspired by the geometrical principles of a deep-sea sponge. The tessellated, net-like weave is based on a point cloud and adapts to the characteristics and proportions of the wearer.

Certain areas, printed with a thermo-chromatic biodegradable polylactic acid (PLA) filament, are sewn into the 3D-printed garment, and change colour based on the mood of the wearer.

LAMELLA AND GILLS

Thin layering systems in organic artefacts are referred to as lamella. The hymenium on the underside of the portobello mushroom has an intricate structural system which consists of elongated lamella. For the 2015 'Sporophyte' ready-to-wear 3D-printed collection, biological artefacts such as flowerless plants which reproduce spores were researched. The term 'sporophyte' refers to a specific stage in the life cycle of a plant that spores are produced. The Hymenium jacket is 3D printed using fused deposition modelling (FDM) PolyJet™ technology by Stratasys Ltd. With this technology a nozzle deposits material on a flat bed. The design is inspired by the structure and performance of organic hymenium topologies, the tissue layer of the fruiting body of a fungus. The three-dimensional structure of this jacket is designed to enhance the performance and flexibility of the garment. The parametric change in the pattern of the gills, from organic to linear, creates an enigmatic see-through effect. It animates the motion of the human body while the lines are performing structurally.

BRANCHING AND INTRICACY

The Kelp jacket, necklace and headpiece are also part of the 2015 'Sporophyte' collection, and likewise use PolyJet technology. The designs are 3D printed in multiple colours as well as rigidity. This means the designs have gradients from soft to hard without changing the digital geometry and physical thickness. The Kelp series is inspired by the structure and performance of organic kelp topologies. The seaweed consists of a complex and intricate layering system. The branching geometry appears to naturally grow on the human body. Implementing growth patterns and imperfections as found in natural formations evokes an organic sensibility.

PLEATS, LEAVES AND TRANSLUCENCY

Orchids, flowers and leaves are inspiring forms in the design process. The organic aesthetic can be realised with digital polygon modelling techniques. This is a digital sculpting process comparable to traditional analog clay modelling. The digital process enables an iterative design methodology where the interactive continuous engagement in developing these organic forms is one of the most exciting aspects related to digital craft. 3D-printing technology allows these highly detailed organic forms and structures to be realised. A drawing by the 19th-century German biologist Ernst Haeckel is the basis of inspiration for the design of the Hybrid Holism 3D-printed dress, a collaboration with Iris van Herpen. The dress was presented in 2012 at Van Herpen's haute couture show in Paris. The organic leaves are in contrast to the underlying structure, which uses a mathematical logic to create a series of pleated fins. This 3D-printed two-piece garment is made possible through a technology known as mammoth stereolithography. In this process a laser fuses material in a liquid resin bath. When introducing texture and three-dimensional curvature, a layering effect similar to a fingerprint is revealed on a micro scale of the surface. The texture is a lightly translucent honey colour. The material is rigid and acts as a protective hard second skin around the body.

Julia Koerner,
Hymenium jacket,
'Sporophyte'
collection,
Sheats Goldstein
Residence,
Los Angeles,
June 2015

The 3D-scanned lamellas and gills of the hymenium of fungi inspired this 3D-printed jacket's morphology. Manufactured by Stratasys Ltd, with PolyJet technology, the jacket synthesises enigmatic 3D effects, structural performance and flexible material logic. Featured in an editorial for *Schön!* magazine, it is combined with gloves from Majesty Black.

Julia Koerner,
Kelp jacket,
'Sporophyte'
collection,
Sheats Goldstein
Residence,
Los Angeles,
June 2015

Intricate woven seaweed found on the coast at Malibu was researched and digitised into a 3D branching system which seems to be growing naturally around the body. The ready-to-wear jacket is manufactured by Stratasys Ltd, where multi-material printing technology was explored.

Julia Koerner in collaboration with Iris van Herpen, Hybrid Holism dress, 2012-13 Fall/Winter Haute-Couture Paris Fashion Week, July 2012

The first collaboration between the architect and fashion designer featured this two-piece honey-coloured 3D-printed dress. Manufactured by Materialise, it utilised the large-scale 3D-printing technique, mammoth stereolithography.

FOLDS, LINES AND LACE

Folding is a technique in garment making where a surface textile is continuously creased, layer by layer, to create a three-dimensional effect. In comparison to traditional handcrafted folding, the digital technique allows for a three-dimensional folding process where any layer can fold into and through another. A second collaboration with Iris van Herpen investigates a new technology known as laser sintering – a technique that uses a flexible, powder-based material which is stretchable and can conform to the movement of the body. A network of thin organic lines are digitally folded and interlaced to create a fragile structural pattern that can flow on the body, in the form of a garment. The lace-like texture animates the wearer's body. The Voltage dress was featured in 2013 at Van Herpen's haute-couture show in Paris. The flexible material is a breakthrough advancement in wearable 3D-printed apparel.

PETALS AND NESTING

The nesting of spaces in architectural design leads to a non-linear programmatic organisation within a building. In fashion design, nesting typically repeats the same part in a linear grid over the form of a body. In a digital design environment, each part can be unique and nested in gradients based on design and performance parameters. This logic reveals both a connectivity and separation between organically grown layers. The 2014 'Biopiracy' ready-to-wear show in Paris featured another collaboration with Iris van Herpen, which experimented with 3D petal forms nested generatively across the human body to create a garment. The design elaborates on the use of laser sintering technology and flexible material. The dress is printed in clusters. It is assembled and sewn with a needle and thread, combining traditional techniques with digital processes. The clusters of petals aggregate parametrically along the body, and have differentiated gradients of thickness. Volumetric petals perform structurally, while thin lightweight petals are nested to create the effect of movement.

SURFACE, SMOCKING AND TEXTURE

Smocking is a technique in garment making where a surface textile is stitched in a specific way to create intricate three-dimensional patterns that have depth and an organic appearance. Undulating concave and convex shapes repeat to create continuity in the overall field. The 3D-printed Smock corset was a collaboration with Marina Hoermanseder that explored the combination of traditional crafted clothing with today's progressive digital techniques. Showcased at the Mercedes-Benz Fashion Week in Berlin in July 2015, it aims to demonstrate the reproduction of traditional garment texturing and forming techniques within the digital design space. The material's rigidity creates a defensive and robust corset that conveys the fluidity and flexibility of a traditional smock corset through its texture, design and accuracy in fabrication. The texture of the smocking is generated parametrically around the body and modelled to a perfect fit.

Julia Koerner in collaboration with Iris van Herpen, Voltage dress, 2013 Spring/Summer Haute Couture Paris Fashion Week, January 2013

The spline-based gradients of lines are digitally generated with visual programming techniques. This pioneering garment is the first of its kind printed in flexible material, manufactured by Materialise in Belgium. The lace pattern performs structurally, while the flow lines visually animate the body's curvature.

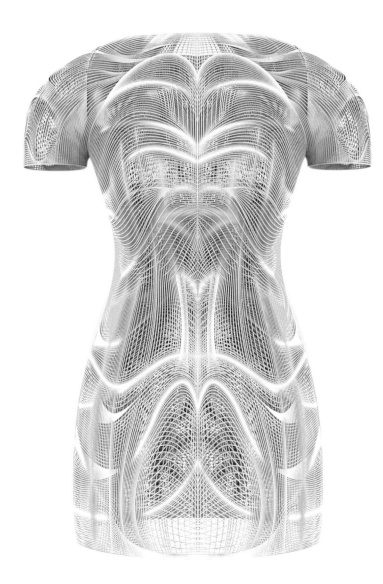

Julia Koerner in
collaboration with
Marina Hoermanseder,
Smock corset,
Mercedes-Benz
Fashion Week,
Berlin,
July 2015

The 3D-printed ready-to-wear corset,
manufactured by Materialise in
Belgium, fuses the architect's highly
technological approach towards
fashion with the fashion designer's
signature leather craftsmanship.
The aim is to explore the translation
of traditional surface texturing and
smocking techniques into digital
generative processes.

THE SYNTHESIS OF DIGITAL AND TRADITIONAL

Additive manufacturing processes exist today in multiple
technologies and materials. Initially used as a prototyping
technique, they are evolving towards manufacturing. Using 3D
printing for the manufacturing of fashion garments unveils a series
of unprecedented opportunities.

Additive manufacturing allows for localised on-site production
of garments, eliminating overseas sweatshops, shipping costs and
associated carbon footprints. Several materials used in 3D printing
are biodegradable and others can be melted, fused and reused.
The accuracy and ability to digitally adapt form allows for highly
customised garments that can be printed on demand, leading to
mass-customisation. Garment sizes as they exist today may become
irrelevant, as the process of individual sizing will be automated
and no two dresses will be identical. Today, the technology still has
limitations in terms of cost, durability and ability to print dissimilar
materials. The optimal use of today's design and fabrication
technology is related to the combination of digital and traditional
craft. This is the future of 3D-printed wearables. ⌂

Notes
1. Marcel Haedrich, *Coco Chanel: Her Life, Her Secrets*, Little, Brown & Company
(Boston, MA), 1979, p 252.
2. Amy Thomas, 'Cheat Sheet | Architectural Fashion', *New York Times* (online),
28 January 2009, http://tmagazine.blogs.nytimes.com/2009/01/28/cheat-sheet-
architectural-fashion/.
3. Michael Pawlyn, *Biomimicry in Architecture*, RIBA Publishing (London), 2011, p 42.

Nervous System,
Kinematics Dress #6,
2015

Although each piece is rigid,
together they act like a
fabric, folding and flowing in
response to body movement.

DRESS

DEMOCRATISING DESIGN THROUGH

Jessica Rosenkrantz and Jesse Louis-Rosenberg

/CODE

COMPUTATION AND DIGITAL FABRICATION

Computer-controlled manufacturing techniques offer the possibility of making bespoke design accessible to all. **Jessica Rosenkrantz and Jesse Louis-Rosenberg**, cofounders of design studio Nervous System in Somerville, Massachusetts, have made some groundbreaking ventures into this new field. Their projects, described here, offer customisation of items such as jewellery, dresses and running shoes through interfaces between specially developed Web apps, body scans and biometric data.

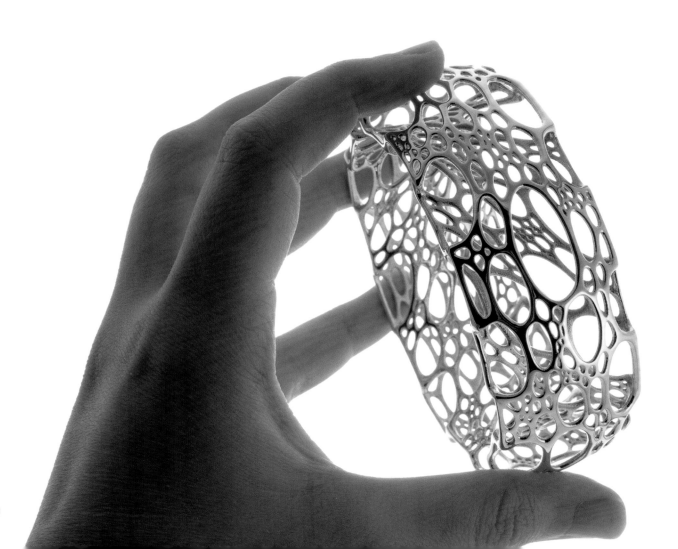

Instead of creating single static designs, Nervous System produces generative products through the coding of playful systems that produce a myriad of results. The products – such as jewellery, clothing, lamps and jigsaw puzzles – are accompanied by Web-based tools that open the design process to customers. The studio's inspiration comes from research into natural systems, computational design and digital fabrication. In architecture, these ideas seem to be speculative futures; the aim of Nervous System is to break these concepts out of academia and into the real world. It is not yet feasible to grow and print buildings, but why not apply such ideas to product design now?

Creating customised products requires fabrication technologies that allow the creation of one-of-a-kind designs for the same cost as cookie-cutter ones. Manufacturing techniques like injection moulding require investment in a single form, making the production of one-off designs financially intractable. Mass production will not work.

Computer-controlled manufacturing techniques like laser cutting and 3D printing open up new possibilities for making. They enable the fabrication of complex objects and make it possible to create one-of-a-kind designs for similar costs to mass-produced ones. These machines – now in offices, public libraries and even homes – put precision manufacturing in the hands of everyone. However, these promises are still more dream than reality. A key part of the equation is missing: software. How do you create the designs? Design software is expensive, difficult to use, and it does not leverage the complexity or variation that digital manufacturing makes possible.

Nervous System creates new types of playful design experiences that leverage simulation, digital fabrication and Web technology to make it possible for anyone to create. Their design systems are inspired by nature's dynamic processes which grow and adapt to different conditions, resulting in unique, adapted forms.

Form as process is a counterpoint to the top-down way by which people usually construct objects. Designers create objects by directly specifying precise measurements and shapes, often determining the essence of the outcome at the beginning. Computers offer new ways of making, but most design software tries to reproduce the methods by which people made things before computers. There is software that gives the experience of drafting, sculpting, or painting. These tools translate how humans have worked with physical materials into a strange digital analog of those experiences. Nervous System proposes a different direction, focusing on the development of interactive processes that people can engage with. Instead of drawing structures, Nervous System is interested in growing them. Instead of creating static designs, it creates dynamic systems.

CELL CYCLE

Cell Cycle (2009) was Nervous System's initial foray into marrying computation and 3D printing to create customised products. It is a jewellery collection and a Web app where anyone can customise their own rings, bracelets or sculpture for 3D printing in plastic or precious metal. In the app, you sculpt a responsive physics simulation of a spring mesh, twisting, morphing and subdividing cells to transform a basic mesh into an intricate, bespoke structure. Cell Cycle was the first online tool for customising 3D-printable products.

The project was inspired by the logic, aesthetics and structural efficiency of radiolarians. Radiolarians create cellular skeletons from silica, using a small amount of material to produce large, strong structures. By applying this logic to the design system, Nervous System created a framework for generating products that can be 3D printed affordably by minimising material volume.

Today mass customisation is a buzzword that evokes cosmetic changes like picking the colours of your tennis shoe. However, customisation has potential to change the way people interact with objects. Nervous System's design apps aim to create experiences that are open-ended and engaging. Users need space to create meaningful variation; not just picking options, but exploring a large design space where their input yields a unique result they are invested in. Apps with multiple levels of engagement, both shallow and deep, accommodate people of different skill levels while still allowing exploration. Someone might begin by making a small tweak, loading a pre-existing design and changing its size, but gradually become absorbed in an in-depth design process. By making it easy for users to save, share and remix designs, Cell Cycle opens up additional entry points into the design process.

Cell Cycle's intuitive interface eschews traditional user-interface (UI) elements like sliders and buttons for direct geometry manipulation. Users push and pull on the structure, morphing it in real time. They subdivide and merge cells to create areas of intricacy or sparseness. As a result, it feels more like playing a game than using a CAD tool. In the background, Cell Cycle ensures that the design is 3D-printable, but not all of the outcomes result in wearable jewellery.

An open-ended design process raises the question, should we allow people to fail? Attempts to mitigate error or frustration often unduly limit the design space. The system leaves open avenues to weird results because closing them would severely limit the space for exploration.

Nervous System,
Custom Cell
Cycle bracelet,
2016

opposite: Nervous System opens up the design process to customers via playful design apps. This sterling silver bracelet cast from 3D-printed wax was co-created by a customer using the Cell Cycle app.

KINEMATICS

Kinematics (2013) is a project that fuses fashion, software and 3D printing to examine how digital fabrication and generative design can impact the way clothing is created. How can 3D printing be used, not just to explore new forms, but to change the way we produce clothing entirely? Can 3D printing make clothes that fit better, customised to one's shape and style? Can it make clothing more efficiently and ethically? Nervous System envisions a new manufacturing workflow where design, simulation and fabrication work in concert.

Bodies are three-dimensional, but clothing is traditionally made from flat material cut and painstakingly pieced together. In contrast, Kinematics garments are created in 3D from body scans and require no assembly. Nervous System employs a smart folding strategy to compress Kinematics garments into a smaller form for efficient fabrication. By folding the garments before printing them, it is possible to make structures larger than a 3D printer that unfold into their intended shape automatically. Kinematics enables the design of custom-fit garments which can be fabricated without anything being cut, sewn or assembled.

The seed of the project grew from considering how 3D printers might be used to create new types of textiles. Textiles are human constructions: raw materials transformed to have completely different behaviours based on how they are arranged in space. The arrangement matters more to how a fabric behaves than the raw material itself. For instance, whether a textile is woven or knitted has more effect on its drape and stretch than whether it is cotton or wool. Geometry begets materiality.

3D printing furthers the possibilities for computationally constructing materials. Complex configurations of matter can result in meta-materials with properties that vary through space. A 3D-printed textile might change in structure across the body to perform distinct functions. 3D printing is commonly used to create hard plastic prototypes. However, by taking advantage of its ability to produce interlocking designs (like a gearbox or chain), it is possible to fabricate parts that behave like soft materials.

Kinematics textiles are based on triangular modules connected by hinges that tessellate a surface. The resulting constructions are a hybrid between soft and hard materials. Although each component is rigid, in aggregate they behave as a continuous fabric, allowing Kinematics garments to flexibly conform and fluidly flow in response to body movement. Unlike traditional fabric, Kinematics textiles are not uniform; they can vary in rigidity, drape, flexibility, porosity and pattern by the applying of different module sizes and types across the body.

The garments created by this process are complex assemblages of thousands of unique articulated parts. These structures would be difficult and time-consuming to create in traditional computer-aided design (CAD) modelling, but Nervous System's Kinematics Cloth app makes design accessible to anyone. Kinematics Cloth is a Web application where people can design custom-fit 3D garments by sketching and sculpting. A variety of clothing items can be created in the app, including dresses, skirts and shirts. Users sculpt the silhouette and hemline of their garment and determine the pattern of the garment's tessellated fabric structure. Kinematics Cloth is built in JavaScript and WebGL.

The design process occurs in real time, using an adaptive re-meshing technique which enables immediate visualisation of user input. Kinematics Cloth builds garments to your exact measurements. Using parametric body modelling technology from

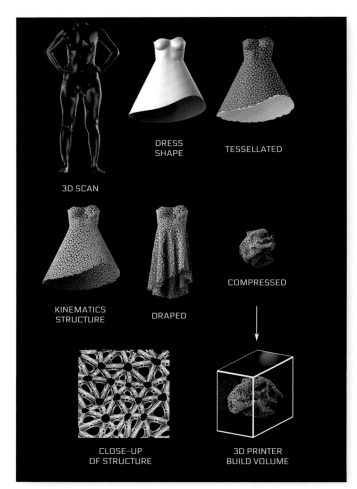

Nervous System,
Kinematics system,
2013

above: The designers proposed a new workflow for creating bespoke clothing that combines body scans, 3D printing and simulation. This dress is computationally folded prior to printing, allowing it to be made in a single piece.

below: The Kinematics Cloth app can be used to create dresses with textile structures that vary across the body. These garments can then be simulated in the Kinematics Fold software to understand how they will drape, fit and move.

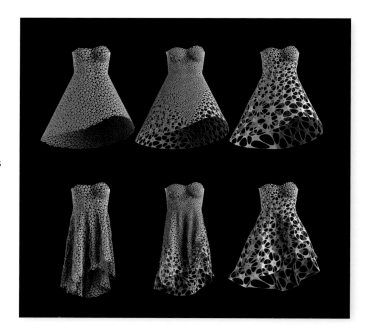

Nervous System,
Kinematics Dress #1,
Museum of Modern Art,
New York,
2014

above: This 3D-printed dress was the culmination of more than a year of research and development combining design, manufacturing and simulation.

top right: 3D printed as a single piece, the dress is composed of over 2,200 triangular panels interconnected by hinges.

bottom right: The dress was printed by selective laser sintering (SLS) in a folded form calculated by the Kinematics Fold software. Technicians at Shapeways excavate the folded garment. The excess nylon powder must be removed before the dress can be unfolded.

Body Labs, users import their own body shape into the app through 3D scanning or traditional measurements. The entire design process takes place in 3D on the customer's own body. There is no flat pattern and no flat representation; what you see is what you get.

Clothing designs generated in Kinematics Cloth are too large to fit in a 3D printer. To make them printable, they must be compressed with Kinematics Fold, Nervous System's simulation tool for Kinematics designs. For example, a Kinematics Dress is compressed by over 85 per cent by folding it in half twice. In addition to using the simulation to optimise for manufacturing, it can also be used to understand how garments will fit, drape and move. This allows designers to have a feedback loop between designing clothes in Kinematics Cloth and understanding how they will behave in Kinematics Fold without ever having to 3D print anything.

Kinematics Fold is based on the idea of simulating the hinged movement of Kinematics designs to compress them digitally. To find a small configuration for fabrication, the system uses a heuristic method involving a rigid body simulation. Finding a mathematically optimal configuration is computationally intractable for an iterative design process; the problem of garment folding shares many similarities with the famously difficult problem of protein folding. Instead, Nervous System computationally folds garments much like you would fold a shirt to put it in a drawer. Each garment goes through a series of collisions designed to reduce the overall size in an intuitive manner.

Rather than simulating the actual geometry of the garment, Kinematics Fold models simplified volumes connected by precise hinge constraints. This accelerates the computation, but comes with associated trade-offs. The folding process is a careful balance of error and precision. The hinges must be manufactured to a high tolerance (within one-tenth of a millimetre) or joints fuse, becoming solid. However, if the simulation is too precise, it can experience locking: modules become stuck in an inefficient configuration. Some error in the system is necessary to realistically mimic the looseness of the joints, and find a small form to print in.

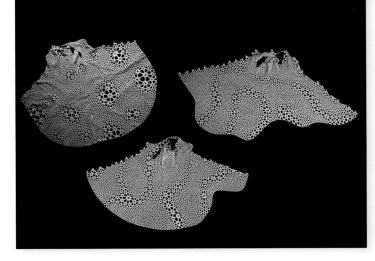

Nervous System,
Kinematics Dresses 2, 4 and 5,
2015

Each 3D-printed dress has a unique shape and pattern customised via an online application to the creator's body shape and preferences.

Nervous System,
Kinematics Petals Dress #1,
Museum of Fine Arts,
Boston,
2016

opposite: Inspired by feathers and scales, this Kinematics dress features a layer of shells which sheathe the body in a directional landscape of overlapping plumes.

below: The Petals dress adds a new layer of customisation to the system. Each element is now individually customisable: varying in direction, length and shape.

These considerations led to a multistage process of compression/folding with a higher error, relaxation with a lower error, and then refitting. Refitting takes a low error configuration and modifies the folded design to ensure no error in the hinge tolerance. However, controlling the error during folding is a difficult process. With complex simulations containing thousands of circular constraints, the error varies with the size of the system and degree of strain, requiring careful tuning. Despite these challenges, Kinematics Fold can compress designs with thousands of interlocking pieces into 3D-print-ready configurations within minutes.

Nervous System imagined Kinematics in 2013, but it was not until the end of 2014 that the studio 3D printed its first dress. It took a year of design, research and development to create a robust textile structure and code the design and simulation applications. Kinematics Dress #1, the culmination of all this work, was 3D printed in September of 2014 at the Shapeways factory in New York City and acquired by the Museum of Modern Art. The dress is a technical achievement, but it is also an article of clothing designed with comfort and durability in mind. Nervous System aimed to make a 3D-printed garment that you can actually wear, one that invites movement instead of constraining it. The result is a custom-fit gown with an intricately patterned structure composed of 2,279 unique triangular panels interconnected by 3,316 hinges, all 3D printed as a single folded piece in nylon.

In 2016, Nervous System produced Kinematics Petals Dress #1 for the Museum of Fine Arts, Boston. Inspired by petals, feathers and scales, Nervous System developed a new textile language for Kinematics where the interconnected elements are articulated as imbricating shells. Petals protrude from the underlying framework of tessellated triangular panels, sheathing the body in a directional landscape of overlapping plumes. Each textile element is now individually customisable: variable in direction, length and shape.

In total, Nervous System has produced more than a dozen unique Kinematics garments. And thousands have created their own Kinematics designs online using the Kinematics Cloth app or have printed custom Kinematics jewellery at home.

Petals
protrude from the
underlying framework
of tessellated
triangular panels,
sheathing the
body in a
directional landscape
of overlapping
plumes

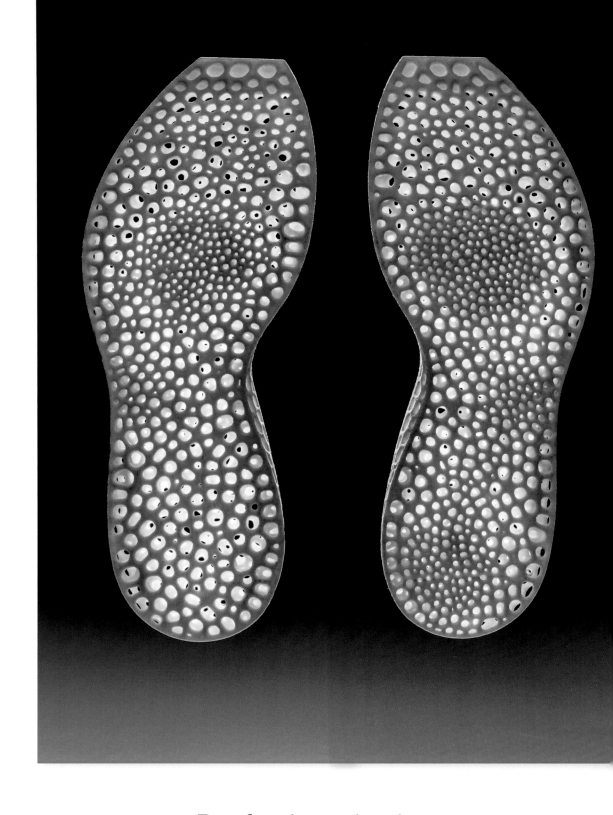

By fusing design,
simulation and manufacturing,
Nervous System invents new types of
design tools that are more powerful,
accessible and democratic.

DATA-DRIVEN DESIGN

The previous projects incorporated user input and body shape into the design of wearables. This project adds a new layer of data on top of the body to create performance footwear with customised function. Nervous System collaborated with New Balance to create the Zante Generate (2016), a running shoe with a midsole 3D printed in a new thermoplastic polyurethane (TPU) elastomer material by selective laser sintering (SLS). Unlike traditional midsoles, these are not a uniform foam, but a structure that can adapt to different runners.

Midsoles are typically made of foam, a material whose structure is a three-dimensional array of cells. Foams have a low relative density and are highly porous, giving them the rare property of being both lightweight and strong. While man-made foams are rather uniform, the foams seen in nature (like wood and bone) are highly variable in scale and direction, enabling specific material properties in different zones.

Inspired by nature's variable-density foams, Nervous System created proprietary systems based on capacity-constrained centroidal Voronoi diagrams to generate midsoles from runners' biometric data, creating variable-density cushioning customised to how a person runs.

Researchers in New Balance's Sports Lab collect pressure data from runners. By placing a sensor inside a shoe, they track how much force is exerted across the foot during a run. Nervous System translates that data into a cellular structure that geometrically adapts to the different forces. By locally increasing cell density, the structure provides more support where more pressure is applied. Cell density can decrease in areas of low force, to minimise the midsoles' weight.

By applying new technologies to everyday products like jewellery, clothing and footwear, Nervous System proposes how such tech can influence the way we construct the world around us and express ourselves. The studio's projects leverage computation and digital fabrication to make design more personal, whether through engagement in the design process or by conforming to an individual's idiosyncrasies. By fusing design, simulation and manufacturing, Nervous System invents new types of design tools that are more powerful, accessible and democratic. ⌂

New Balance,
Zante Generate,
2016

below: Nervous System collaborated with New Balance to create performance running shoes with customisable, 3D-printed midsoles.

opposite: The midsoles' foam structure can be geometrically adapted to an individual's body via pressure data. The left midsole is for someone who strikes with their forefoot; the right is for a runner who strikes with their heel.

Text © 2017 John Wiley & Sons Ltd. Images: pp 48–9, 53(tr&b), 55 © Steve Marsel Studio; pp 50–2, 53(tl), 54 © Jessica Rosenkrantz, Nervous System; pp 56–7 © New Balance Athletics, Inc

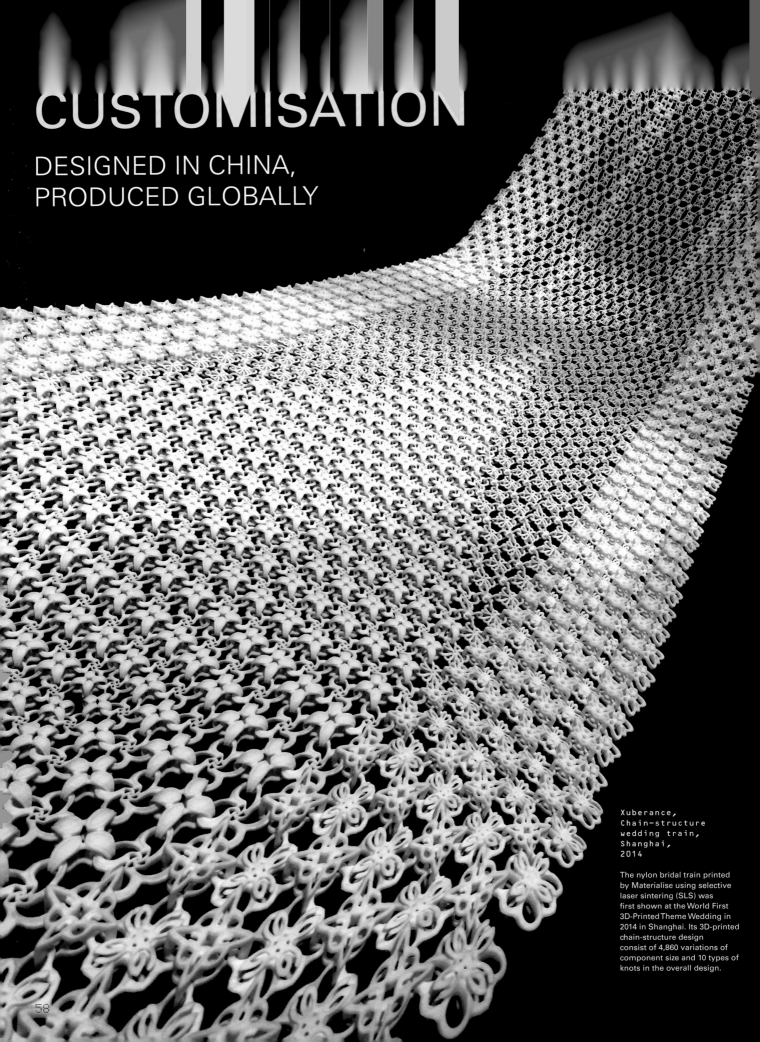

CUSTOMISATION

DESIGNED IN CHINA,
PRODUCED GLOBALLY

Xuberance,
Chain-structure
wedding train,
Shanghai,
2014

The nylon bridal train printed
by Materialise using selective
laser sintering (SLS) was
first shown at the World First
3D-Printed Theme Wedding in
2014 in Shanghai. Its 3D-printed
chain-structure design
consist of 4,860 variations of
component size and 10 types of
knots in the overall design.

Steven Ma

Given the right level of creativity and entrepreneurship, designing for customised 3D printing can offer highly profitable business opportunities anywhere in the world. Xuberance is a case in point. Set up in Shanghai in 2014, the firm's innovative approach to working in both business-to-business and consumer markets has earned it huge international recognition and commercial success in an astoundingly short time. Cofounder and Chief Design Officer **Steven Ma** outlines the journey so far.

With the increasing role of 3D printing, digital scanning, and various other technologies which shorten and simplify the manufacturing process, the value of design becomes ever more important. As has been seen in so many cases, the development of applications for 3D printing begins with the designers.

Xuberance is a 3D-printing design brand based in Shanghai that is dedicated to offering a personalised service for high-end customisation projects. Set up in 2014, its three founding partners – myself as Chief Design Officer, Bin Lu as Chief Sales Officer and Leirah Wang as Chief Executive Officer – all have a background in architecture. The team has since expanded into a mid-size international 3D-printing design company with over 30 employees. Xuberance's long-term goal is to create the best 3D-printing design brand in Asia, by providing a direct-to-customer/client design service with 3D printing as a solution for mass customisation. At the time of writing, it is still the only 3D-printing design company in China centred on both consumer products and business-to-business (B2B) personalised projects. Xuberance also runs retail shops and cafes for offline 3D-printing experiences.

In 2016 Xuberance launched its own Inno Design Centre, which focuses on educational design training, intellectual property rights (IPR) trading services, a digital database library, robotic printing research and development. The idea is to provide a platform for collaboration between various institutes, universities and local governments, creating dialogues between education and digital design production with additive manufacturing technologies. The outcomes of the research can be commercialised to become products for investors interested in capitalising on it. As a non-profit project, contributing to the 3D-printing industry in China, early in 2017 Xuberance opened the first China 3D-Printing Cultural Museum in Shanghai, which promotes additive manufacturing with a fully equipped 5,000-square-metre (54,000-square-foot) facility including 3D-printing service centre, materials library, exhibition space, conference halls, maker spaces, children's learning centre, cafe and shops. It is China's largest additive manufacturing development complex.

Xuberance is not only interested in designing art pieces and exhibition installations. The company has found the balance between the cost-effective solution of 3D printing and the real demands of the market. It has opened up a sustainable business strategy for customised projects that employ environmentally friendly production methods, through the use of additive manufacturing. To offer a complete ecosystem and ensure sustainable growth of the business model, the 3D-printing industry in China needs to fuse manufacturing/service, design/product, capital/investor and channel/markets.

FROM 'MADE IN CHINA' TO 'CREATED IN CHINA'

In China the 21st century is not only the century of technology, but also increasingly an age of creativity and design. New technologies – such as 3D printing – even accelerate this trend, giving limitless possibilities to designers. However, for designers there is an inherent challenge in creating 3D-printing products which can be easily distributed, copied and sold. Especially in China's markets, a strong intellectual property framework recognising the embedded value of design and creative innovation in 3D-printing products would be highly beneficial to young design startups, helping them confidently enter the market and encouraging them to collaborate with each other. The diverse range of output materials and the development of the latest

Xuberance,
Peace Hotel,
Shanghai,
2014

Xuberance's first office, on the second floor of the Peace Hotel on Shanghai's Bund, with 50 square metres (540 square feet) of space. This creative lounge acts as a combination of showroom, design office and printing lab. Leirah Wang (CEO of Xuberance) holds a newly developed 3D-printed flexible chain-structure lampshade.

Xuberance 3D Cafe,
Shanghai,
2017

above: A new Xuberance 3D Cafe designed with 3D-printed ceiling installation 'SKYLINES' series opened on 5 May 2017 at DNA Coffice at 480 YongJia Road, Xuhui District, Shanghai.

Xuberance,
'Lush & Luna' series,
Shanghai,
2016

right: The 3D-printed metal chopsticks and ceramic plate were the best-selling consumer products among other Xuberance 3D-printed product lines in 2016, sold through multiple online platforms and offline cafes and shops in China.

3D-printing technologies have inspired design aesthetics and strengthened the concept of the important role that 3D printing will play in the future. Designers can now easily customise their own 3D-printed designs. With the exponential growth of advanced materials development over the past two years, the field has matured enough to allow materialisation of any form imaginable through the process of additive manufacturing. Designers can now switch their focus towards higher aesthetic value and customised design. The developments have also opened the door to an entirely new level of possible complexity, allowing digitally sculpted forms to be realised by 3D printing, and have enhanced the idea of 'manufacturing for design'.

In China, 3D printing has become increasingly popular in recent years as an easy, cost-effective solution for creating real parts from digital data. The Chinese government has played a significant role in bringing about the boom of the additive manufacturing industry since 2012. In the light of the 'Made in China 2025' strategy that it recently launched to promote innovative manufacturing approaches, many cities have opened their own 3D-printing service centres and promoted additive manufacturing with expos and events all year round. One well-known additive manufacturing company, Materialise, headquartered in Belgium, also set up a China-region office in Shanghai, focused on software development and educational activities for young children. Since 2014, the Xuberance team have been working with Materialise on several significant projects which would not previously have been possible with local companies due to a lack of software support or the experience of printing heavy digital data files. Printing services provided by local companies were not as professional as those outsourced internationally in the early days.

DESIGN AS A SERVICE
From early 2012, many companies in China tried to replicate the success of New York-based 3D-printing firm Shapeways, founded in 2007 and now with factories also in Eindhoven and Seattle. The business model involved using an online-to-offline platform to provide a direct service, from order to print to delivery. Unfortunately all these Chinese companies failed, due to the non-mature market of users in the early years of 3D-printing

Xuberance, 'Wedding' series, Shanghai, 2014

World First 3D-Printed Theme Wedding was held on 12 December 2014 at Shanghai Concert Hall. Multiple 3D-printed materials were used to produce many products in this event, including a 3D-printed wedding dress, bridal flowers, cakes, jewellery, lights and accessories.

development in the country, as well as the lack of designers working in this field, which caused low usage of the online platforms. China was still at the educational stage of additive manufacturing for the general public in 2014. It needed a new business model to evolve, reflecting local interests and its own markets.

Recently, many companies have been turning their focus to additive manufacturing, leading sales of machines to triple in just a year. Additive manufacturing technologies and the related business model have been developing for more than two decades in America and Europe; yet China, where 3D-printing businesses have only emerged over the last five years, has already caught up. Rapid economic growth in Chinese cities brought about tremendous opportunities. Machines owned by Chinese companies became overloaded, and one of the key problems that resulted from this was that content development was almost ignored. In order to showcase what their machines were capable of printing, these companies often downloaded models and copies of other designs. Originality was missing, while what almost all these companies needed was innovative products. Content design (digital data) and service design also play a significant role in creating the ecosystem linking service providers and clients that is needed for consumers to access 3D printing. It helps them easily to fulfil their design needs, to create products that are special and that have never appeared on the market before. 'Mass customisation' can become reality: everyone wants to be different.

With several years of development, many industries have now utilised 3D-printing technologies due to their quick turnaround time and their ability to produce stunning projects within tight budgets. As is often seen on an industrial level, typical applications for additive manufacturing include conceptual models, ergonomic studies, visual analysis, form-fit-and-function testing, engineering evaluation and functional testing. But consumer-level products and personalised design for additive manufacturing are still areas that are not fully developed in the Chinese market. It will be the biggest market for additive manufacturing when consumer products are ready to be sold to everyone.

INTELLECTUAL PROPERTY RIGHTS (IPR) TRADING

All new applications, including aerospace, fashion, medicine and industry, start from the creation of a digital design. Without design and the adequate protection of the designer's intellectual property (IP), no sustainable growth or innovation is possible. This is true for conventional manufacturing but especially for additive manufacturing. Every partner in the process wants to protect their designs, solutions, software, materials and hardware to bring new applications to the market that – through 3D printing – can improve the world we are living in, both on a personal level and for the benefit of the whole community.

The 3D-printing business model in Asia, and especially in the China region, is very different from that in North America or Europe. Xuberance's success since 2014 – which has included completion of over 100 customised projects and products with visionary clients throughout China, including Shanghai Tower Group, China Eastern Airlines, Wanke, Starbucks China, Harper's Bazaar Jewelry and Ping An Insurance, among others – demonstrates this different business model.

Between 2014 and 2016, the IPR for Xuberance's 38 3D-printed design products were registered in China in a collaboration with Shanghai's East China University of Political Science and Law to develop an online and office platform for digital copyright trading. One of the registered products – a digital model for the 'Cloud' series of lamps – was sold to a China-based company for 3.2 million Chinese yuan. It marked the first case in the world of a 3D-printed product being traded with such a high value. The Xuberance IPR projects and platform constitute yet another significant milestone in the overall development of the 3D-printing ecosystem in China to support the use of 3D-printing technology to promote design innovation and creativity. They represent an innovation in the business model which serves as a new standard and role model for the rest of the market, and that will in turn spur artists and designers to embrace the technology, knowing that the value of their creation is respected and protected. We are living in a dynamic and changing world, in which the rules and definitions of authorship are in flux, and as designers we are now producing concepts that can be replicated with absolute precision through digital manufacturing. It is not only about the physical products any more, but about control of the idea through controlling intellectual property – no different from a musician or a writer. This opens up a whole new world of opportunities.

CUSTOMISED BUSINESS-TO-BUSINESS (B2B) PROJECTS

Xuberance B2B projects are divided into four main categories: Architecture/Interior & Exhibition, Movie/Entertainment & IP Products, Business Identity Gifts/Products & Trophy Design, and Lighting Design & Furniture.

From 2014 to 2016, 7 tons of nylon powder were used for additive manufacturing through selective laser sintering (SLS) in Xuberance's office. This represents materials costs of approximately 3 million Chinese yuan per year. Materials for the firm's B2B projects are an ongoing expense that will continue to grow annually as more projects come in. In view of this, the team has entered collaborations with many 3D-printing service providers in China, based on how much Xuberance will have printed per year in exchange for an equivalent value in design project fees for their needs. This allows Xuberance to continue to get more B2B projects from its suppliers and at the same time

Xuberance,
Lunamoth stool,
Milan,
2016

This 3D-printed stool, first displayed at SaloneSatellite in Milan in 2016, is a furniture design exploration that combines 3D-printed components with wooden elements. It was one of the products representing Shanghai Industrial Design Association to be exhibited at the International Contemporary Furniture Fair in New York in 2016.

Xuberance,
'Tang' series,
Shanghai,
2016

The 'Tang' series is a wireless light system SLS printed in nylon, measuring 12 by 12 by 15 centimetres (4¾ by 4¾ by 5⅞ inches). It won the Shanghai Industrial Design Association's Innovation Materials Award in 2017, and is now sold all over the world.

generate new business for the company. Xuberance has become the first choice as a design brand to provide design services for 3D-printing solutions in China.

Of Xuberance's employees, 70 per cent are in sales and 20 per cent are designers. The sales manager can generate 3 million Chinese yuan per quarter, with 12–15 million yuan of project value per year in B2B projects where 40 per cent profit is requested for each project. With this setup, the company began making profit in the first quarter of 2016 and increasingly sustained it throughout the entire year. As the sales teams grows, the design team expands proportionally. Its structure is very similar to that of traditional architecture studios, individually running projects and providing direct design services to clients. Most of Xuberance's projects are limited to three weeks from start to completion. By the third quarter of 2017 this design service had started to expand into the Hong Kong and Korean market. Korea also has recently shown exponential growth in the use of 3D printing; but it is still two to three years behind in development compared to China, which will remain the largest market for 3D-printing design services in Asia for years to come.

DIGITAL FUTURE

Today the widespread use of advanced digital design tools and techniques of digital sculpting is encouraging architects to envisage projects that exceed the boundaries of their practice. They are now developing a practice which stands at the crossroads of design, computer science, engineering and biology. Conditions for

Xuberance,
Duality,
Los Angeles,
2016

Duality is a single-printed SLS tea table, 40 by 40 by 70 centimetres (16 by 16 by 28 inches). It was exhibited in the 'Close-Up' exhibition at the Southern California Institute of Architecture (SCI-Arc) gallery in Los Angeles, which examined the impact of digital technologies' ability to design objects through continuous degrees of magnification.

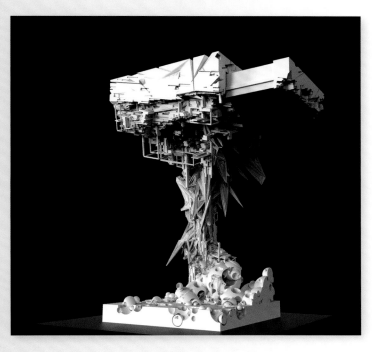

production in the domain of architecture are radically redefined by this convergence, as well as by the constant evolution of processes and tools for digital manufacturing. The more advanced the technology has become, the more refined and sophisticated the detailing of 3D printing, and the greater the possibility for varying the sizes of 3D-printed objects, from ever smaller to ever larger. In other words, 3D printing is gradually approaching customised human body scale, even in close contact with the human body, as prostheses are commonly used. With the latest developments, 3D printing is no longer just an experimental tool or representational model, but in all aspects can be employed at a high level of application customised to the human body, such as dental appliances, healthcare devices, bone substitutions, fashion wearables, furniture and food applications, and so on. The combination of additive manufacturing technology and digital design techniques also creates the ambition to establish conditions beyond the usual, the known, the rational, the obvious and the simple. The use of 3D printing and the idea of 'digital sculpturism' allow designers to emphasise the artistic and the expressive possibilities of arts and architecture. This also reflects general excitement, enthusiasm, energy and high spirits, because the richness of its content suggests unique and potent elements. Xuberance's work rests on the potentialities of digital tools distanced from any attempt at optimisation, in favour of baroque, excessive and abundant aesthetics. ᗐ

Xuberance,
3D-printed wall,
Shanghai,
2016

This 5-by-1.8-metre (16-by-6-foot) wall was 3D-printed with white polylactic acid (PLA) materials in 108 pieces assembled together. It is a customised interior project for a cafe wall shelf design with changeable-colour light system installed.

Francis Bitonti,
Chromat Adrenaline
Dress, New York,
2016

The Chromat Adrenaline
Dress, powered by
Intel's Curie module, is
composed of 3D-printed
panels and an interlinked,
expandable carbon-
fibre framework. When
the garment senses
adrenaline, the dress's
framework mimics the
human fight-or-flight
mode and extends to
form an imposing shape.

MICROMECHANICAL ASSEMBLIES AND THE HUMAN BODY

Zaha Hadid
for United Nude,
Flames,
2015

Hadid's design for the Re-Inventing Shoes
collaboration was informed by the flickering light
of fire. Flame-like bands originate from the point of
the heel, rising upwards to gently embrace the foot,
while the ergonomically optimised foot bed provides
comfort and support.

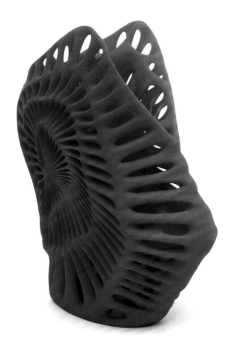

Ben van Berkel
for United Nude,
UNX2,
2015

Part of the collaborative Re-Inventing Shoes project, the aim of the UNX2 shoe was to dress the foot in such a way as to make its form partially visible, to highlight the mechanics of the foot and the visual effects that can be created by the shoe in motion.

Fernando Romero
for United Nude,
Ammonite,
2015

The design of this shoe, part of the Re-inventing Shoes project, finds its beginning at the intersection of the geometry of nature, the human body, and the cosmos. It uses the most cutting-edge 3D-printing technology both in design and execution, but the result is a shoe that could have been an object found in nature, a delicate fossil buried on the bottom of the ocean for millennia.

Michael Young
for United Nude,
Young Shoe,
2015

The process and material allowed the designers to create the unique lattice work that builds upwards around the heeled shoe to produce a boot with the tactility of lacework that is in fact both durable and flexible at the same time.

Ross Lovegrove
for United Nude,
Ilabo,
2015

The filaments or hairs for the shoe were modelled using particle systems and attraction-repulsion logistics paralleling the bionic geometry of the foot. The complex tridimensional polygon mesh provides a watertight geometry whereby nothing is extraneous either in material volume or functional characteristic.

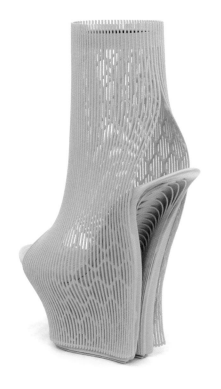

SHOES AS ARCHITECTURE

Following the Re-Inventing Shoes project, a series of interviews were conducted with the designers with whom we had collaborated. Each was asked what connections they could see between shoes and architecture. On the one hand, Fernando Romero thinks that there are a very few connections: 'It's like comparing a long summer abroad with a short trip to propose to your fiancée. Both are nice experiences, but you can't really compare them. The challenges are different, the programmes are different, the ergonomics and timing are different, the desires that should be satisfied by the form are different.'[1] While Ben van Berkel had appreciated our collaboration, he also draws a clear distinction, seeing shoes as more directly related to the human body: '[Creating a pair of shoes] is also of course related more directly to the body compared to architecture, and the way the body moves.'[2]

Zaha Hadid said she enjoyed fashion and shoes precisely because they capture the mood of the moment, and are more instantaneous than the process of designing and constructing buildings: 'I'm into fashion and shoes because they contain the mood of the day, of the moment – like music, literature and art – whereas architecture is a very long process from the start of a project to its completion.' Moreover, she pointed out a clear connection between shoes and buildings: 'Fashion and architecture can be considered as components within a single system of design. The immersive experience of a building can be likened to the tactile sensations of wearing a garment or an accessory. Just as clothing is based on the proportions of the human body, architecture must also be structured in relation to the human scale.'[3]

So can shoes be architecture? This remains an open question. What is abundantly clear, however, is that architects are quite capable of designing elegant shoes. Not only that, but we have shown that an architect can establish a company to reinvent shoes by challenging conventions and breaking the rules. Although, if the truth be known, we ended up breaking the rules not for the sake of it, but simply by not knowing them. ◫

Francis Bitonti,
United Nude
and 3D Systems,
Mutatio Shoe,
2015

The project is a speculation on the future of customisation. Each shoe in the edition is unique, generated by an algorithm developed by the designer. The shoe has a gold-plated SLS 3D-printed heel and a leather upper.

Notes
1. Quote from unpublished United Nude interview with Fernando Romero, spring 2016.
2. Quote from unpublished United Nude interview with Ben van Berkel, spring 2016.
3. Quote from unpublished United Nude interview with Zaha Hadid, spring 2016.

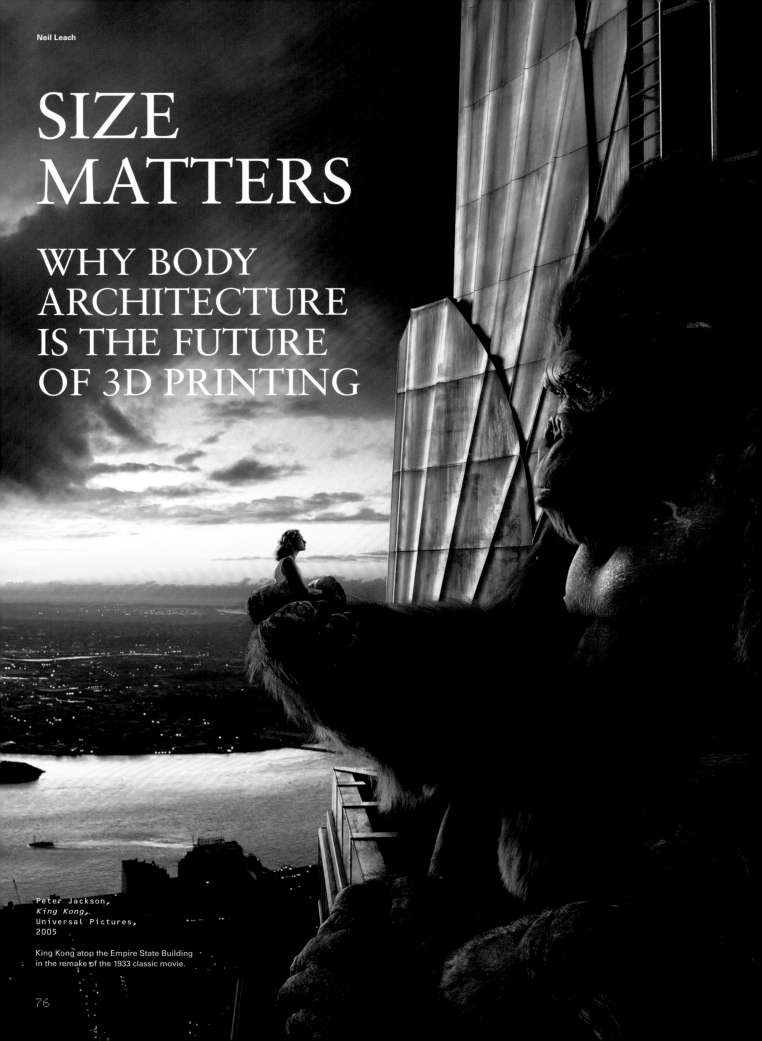

Neil Leach

SIZE MATTERS

WHY BODY ARCHITECTURE IS THE FUTURE OF 3D PRINTING

Peter Jackson,
King Kong,
Universal Pictures,
2005

King Kong atop the Empire State Building
in the remake of the 1933 classic movie.

Computational drafting allows architects to zoom in and out of their creations-in-progress as never before. However, when it comes to digital fabrication processes, changes in scale can have insurmountable implications in terms of structural stability and load bearing – as Guest-Editor **Neil Leach** explains here. Therefore, he argues, rather than dreaming of scaling up 3D printing to the dimension of buildings and cities, architects do better to focus their enthusiasm for this new technology on smaller-scale areas of their practice.

Charles and Ray Eames, *Powers of Ten: A Film Dealing with the Powers of Ten and the Relative Size of Things in the Universe*, IBM, 1977

The movie begins with a scene of a couple enjoying a picnic in Chicago, before zooming out and then zooming back in.

Architects often dream of 3D printing entire buildings. In some cases they dream of 3D printing entire cities.[1] But realistically, what is the future of 3D printing? What are the implications of scaling up? And what are the consequences of the fact that architects often focus on purely visual concerns at the expense of other important constraints? This article explores the ramifications of this in terms of not only material concerns, such as structural performance, but also the economic viability of 3D printing. It concludes that for the moment, at least, the greatest potential of 3D printing lies not in the fabrication of buildings, but in far more modest scales of operation, such as body architecture.

From Jewellery to Cities

One of the hallmarks of architectural production today is the seemingly effortless way in which certain architectural practices find themselves designing at a range of different scales. Alongside their buildings and urban proposals, for example, Greg Lynn FORM designs silverware and boats, UNStudio designs furniture and 3D-printed shoes, and Zaha Hadid Architects designs jewellery, shoes and handbags. But what allows these architects to shift so easily from small-scale to large-scale designs?

In their documentary film *Powers of Ten: A Film Dealing with the Powers of Ten and the Relative Size of Things in the Universe* (1977),[2] American designers Charles and Ray Eames explore relative magnitudes. The opening scene depicts a couple having a picnic in a park viewed from one metre away, zooms out progressively by powers of ten to a distance of 100 million light years, and then zooms back in again right down to 0.00001 ångströms – the scale of quarks, the units of which atoms are composed.

Powers of Ten speaks of its times. The original sketch version was produced in 1968. In macroscopic terms, this was just one year before Neil Armstrong and Buzz Aldrin became the first human beings to walk on the surface of the Moon, and five years after Maarten Schmidt discovered what were to become known as 'quasars'.[3] In microscopic terms this was four years after the quark model was proposed independently by two physicists, Murray Gell-Mann and George Zweig, and three years after the first atom probe was introduced by Erwin Wilhelm Müller and John A Panitz.[4] It was a period in which knowledge of the universe was expanding rapidly at both ends of the visual spectrum.

But what is the relevance of this movie for architects? *Powers of Ten* is a visual representation of the universe perceived at different scales and premised on the notion of 'zooming in' and 'zooming out' that echoes the way in which architects perceive the world in our computational era. Whereas in the old days of parallel motion drawing boards a fixed scale would be selected in advance – 1:10, 1:50, 1:100, 1:200 and so on – with the drawing drafted according to that scale, in our contemporary age of computational drafting, scale as such is not fixed. Rather, computational drafting relies on the same logic of zooming in and zooming out. It is only when a 2D drawing or a 3D model has to be printed out that the size needs to be specified. As such, it could be argued, scale is no longer the fixed constraint that it used to be, and this capacity to zoom in and zoom out is a contributory factor in allowing architects today to design so effortlessly at a range of different scales from jewellery through to cities. But what is at stake in this culture of zooming in and zooming out? Are there material constraints being overlooked? Are economic issues being glossed over? And what implications might these questions have for 3D printing?

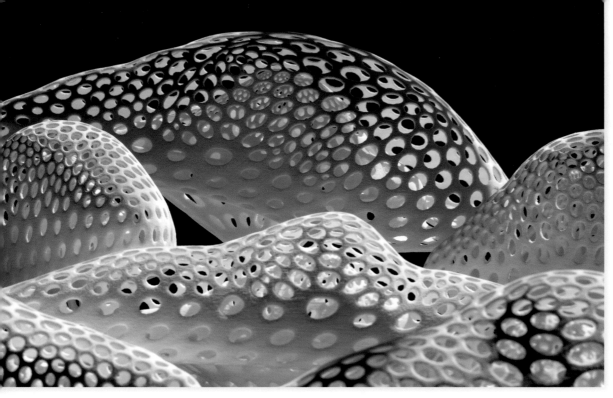

Mamou-Mani Architects,
Overcast,
Victoria and
Albert Museum,
London,
2012

The installation consists of a series of very light 3D-printed plaster 'cloudlets' on a cantilevered steel support. A further example of body-scale 3D-printed objects designed by architects.

The result is that, if scaled up, a creature 10 times the size would be incapable of moving around. Put simply, nature could not produce such a creature. King Kong is a complete fiction.

Mamou-Mani Architects,
Component for Xintiandi
3D Printing Pop-Up
Studio,
Shanghai,
2014

Close-up of the Delta Tower 3D printer and the component being printed with Chinese characters. The installation is part of a series of projects by the architects exploring the potential of small-scale 3D printing.

Out of Scale

One of the interesting aspects of *Powers of Ten* is that, although it starts at 1:1 scale with a life-size scene of a couple relaxing in an outdoor setting, it then zooms out to embrace the whole universe, before zooming back in. However, as it zooms back in it does not stop at the human scale, but transgresses that threshold, and shifts right down to the level of quarks. It is as though there is a form of slippage, and – somewhat disturbingly – we lose our sense of being anchored in the 1:1 scale from which the movie began.

Some sense of the potential shock that results from this loss of scale can be found in various historical books, such as *Gulliver's Travels* (1726) and *Alice's Adventures in Wonderland* (1865), through to movies such as *King Kong* (1933, 2005), *Godzilla* (1954), *Honey, I Shrunk the Kids* (1989), along with the most recent: *Kong: Skull Island* (2017).[5] The sheer number of these books and movies betrays a deep-rooted anxiety about problems incurred by the potential loss of scale. In each case there is something unnatural about the shift in scale that leaves human beings either as midgets or giants struggling to deal with their disproportionately large or small surroundings.

Learning from Biology

Size matters. Ask any biologist. Let us make a comparison between an ant and an elephant. Why does an ant have proportionately long, spindly legs, while an elephant has broad, sturdy legs?[6] In order to answer this question, we might start, perhaps, with the simple mathematical principle that if we double the dimensions of an object, we do not double the volume. Rather the volume increases by a factor of eight. Take, for example, a cube measuring 10 x 10 x 10 centimetres. Its overall volume would be 1,000 cubic centimetres. If we were to double the dimensions of the cube so that it now measures 20 x 20 x 20 centimetres, some might expect the volume of the new, larger cube to be 2,000 cubic centimetres, double that of the original cube. But in fact the volume of the new enlarged cube will be 8,000 cubic centimetres, eight times the volume of the original cube. In other words, as we increase dimensions, so volume increases exponentially.

In terms of an ant, this factor has a number of significant implications not least for its respiratory system. From the perspective of architects, however, the most important consideration is perhaps structural performance. According to the logic outlined above, if the dimensions of an ant were to be doubled, its volume would be increased by a factor of eight. Its weight would likewise increase by a factor of eight. And yet if the intrinsic strength of its skeletal structure also remains the same, the ratio between strength and weight would be reduced. This has serious consequences for the structural performance of the skeletal structure of an ant, and explains why we do not see ants the size of elephants. It also explains why an elephant – as a much larger creature – has proportionately more sturdy legs. Interestingly, research has also shown that the metabolic rate of insects is much more rapid than that of humans, so that time appears much slower.[7] Hence a fly often has little difficulty avoiding a human being trying to swat it. Put simply, to a fly a human being would appear as lumbering and slow, as an elephant appears to a human being.

Let us turn our attention to the example of King Kong atop the Empire State Building. If King Kong were to be 10 times the size of a standard gorilla, then clearly his weight would be 1,000 times greater than that of a standard gorilla. This would

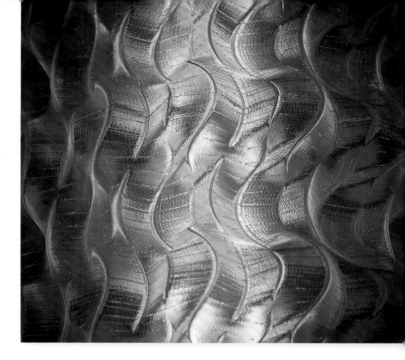

Mamou-Mani Architects,
Cloud Capsule,
London,
2014

This 2-metre (6.5-foot) tall micro-pavilion demonstrates changes in the levels of light suffused through its form. It was designed using Radiance daylight-simulation software, and 'Silkworm', an open-source plug-in for Rhino developed by a team including the architect.

make King Kong intolerably heavy for his structural frame. Thus the images of King Kong atop the Empire State Building are a complete fallacy. It is not a question of whether the Empire State Building could support the weight of a super-enlarged guerilla. No, King Kong could not even support his own weight. The problem is that most animals are 'designed' to carry their own weight – but not much more – in vigorous activity. If scaled up, however, that weight becomes exponentially greater, while the strength of their bones remains the same. As Michael Fowler notes: 'The intrinsic strength of the material bone is made from in animals of all sizes (Calcium apatite embedded in a matrix of collagen) is about the same. The strength of a bone is proportional to its cross sectional area. Compressive failure occurs for a stress of about 2*108 N/m2 (29,000 lbs/in2).'[8] The result is that, if scaled up, a creature 10 times the size would be incapable of moving around. Put simply, nature could not produce such a creature. King Kong is a complete fiction.

So what of the Empire State Building itself? Clearly the same logic would apply. A crucial factor that allowed the New York skyscraper to be built in the first place was the introduction of steel as a building material. After all, it is well known that brick buildings are not constructed to any great height – unless they have some structural steel framework, and brick is used only for cladding.[9] But what is less well known is that the structural constraints of scaling-up the Empire State Building are similar to those of scaling-up a gorilla. Both are governed by the same principles. The intrinsic strength of steel remains the same. Thus, if the Empire State Building were to be scaled-up proportionately 10 times – like King Kong – it would not stand up, unless its

Lei Yu, Arachne 3D-printed building facade,
Foshan, China, 2017

Here, the large-scale non-structural cladding panels have been
3D printed using fused deposition modelling.

Co-de-iT and digifabTURINg,
inFORMed clay matter research project,
2017

The robotic-driven clay deposition is enabled by custom-written
algorithms for the robotic-arm behaviour and a bespoke end-
effector designed to introduce anisotropy and lamination effects,
whose expression is controlled via the robot wrist rotation along
the extrusion path. Clay has proved to be a popular and cheap
medium in the field of 3D-printed body architecture.

structural performance could be improved. Either its structural
frame would have to be fabricated from material with considerably
greater structural properties, or its structural logic would have
to be reconfigured. An example of the latter is the way in which
the simple compressive masonry bridge changed both its material
and structural logic to evolve into large-span steel suspension
bridges, such as the Golden Gate Bridge in San Francisco. One
might surmise, too, that other factors would need to be addressed.
For example, if the respiratory system of an insect does not work
for larger creatures, how would the ventilation, heating and
air-conditioning systems of the Empire State Building need to be
reconfigured if it were to be scaled up? While the Empire State
Building can be scaled down to make popular souvenirs easily
enough, it cannot be scaled up so easily.

This brings us back to *Powers of Ten* and – by extension – the
inherent problem of using computational drafting tools that permit
architects to zoom in and zoom out so effortlessly. While these
tools allow architects to operate seamlessly at a range of scales,
the problem is that they rely on purely visual criteria. The problem
clearly extends to 3D printing, where the inherent strength of the
material – like King Kong's bones or the steel used in the Empire
State Building – remains the same, despite the increase in size.

We can introduce here the distinction that Manuel DeLanda
– following Gilles Deleuze – makes between 'extensive' and
'intensive' properties. Extensive properties refer to mainly visual
properties, such as size, shape and so on, whereas intensive
properties refer to often non-visual properties, such as temperature,
pressure, gravity, tension and compression.[10] These differences
are articulated in a typical weather chart, where visual aspects
such as mountains, rivers and coastlines are extensive features,
whereas non-visual aspects (high- or low-pressure systems, and
warm or cold fronts) are intensive features. The problem with
architects, it could be claimed, is that they are primarily 'extensive'
thinkers in their approach to design. In other words, they focus
mainly on purely visual aspects of form, often to the exclusion of
non-visual behaviours that help to define that form. This kicks in
especially when it comes to the issue of proportionality. If, instead
of subscribing to the logic of proportions whereby architects
scale-up designs in purely visual terms, they were to understand
proportionality as a deep relationality between a design and the
material conditions that generated it, they would understand more
clearly why King Kong could not exist and why architectural
designs cannot be scaled up so effortlessly.

The lesson is clear. In scaling up or down, architects need to step
beyond their ocularcentric approach that privileges the visual, and
take into account other, often invisible, factors.

The Constraints of 3D Printing

What, then, is the consequence of all this? Firstly, and most
obviously, it is clear that architects cannot simply scale up their
designs without taking into account intensive considerations such
as structural concerns. Equally it should be recognised that it would
be impossible to re-create the performance of a full-size building
through a scaled-down model, and vice versa, even if that model
were composed of the same materials as the full-size building.

This has radical implications for 3D printing in particular. Not
only do 3D-printed models not share the same properties as a full-
size building, but the structural performance of 3D-printed objects
is also compromised when they are scaled up. As such, large-scale
3D-printed components can only be used as cladding members,

SHoP Architects,
Flotsam & Jetsam,
Design Miami,
Florida,
2016

above: The installation
consists of the largest
structures ever 3D printed.
It has since been reinstalled
permanently at Jungle Plaza
in the Miami Design District.

left: The structure being
printed using Branch
Technology's innovative
Cellular Fabrication freeform
3D-printing process.

Not only do 3D-printed models not share the
same properties as a full-size building, but the
structural performance of 3D-printed objects
is also compromised when they are scaled up

LACE by Jenny Wu,
Allegro cuff,
2016

The 14-carat rose-gold-plated Allegro cuff expands on Oyler Wu Collaborative's interest in line-based geometry through the digital crafting of this wearable piece. By stacking three thickened 'lines' in space, and applying techniques of chamfering and creasing, the Allegro merges these three subtle variations of the line to form the cuff.

LACE by Jenny Wu,
Catena necklace,
2017

One of the first fully 3D-printed necklaces in metal to utilise binder-jetting technology. It consists of six hinged stainless-steel/bronze pieces and a fully integrated 3D-printed latch. The final piece is bead blasted and finished with a black patina.

It is fairly clear that while 3D printing remains so expensive, its greatest potential lies in 1:1 body-scale production. The lesson here is that size matters.

as in the case of the Arachne facade project designed by Chinese architect Lei Yu (Foshan, China, 2017). Alternatively, for example in the *Flotsam & Jetsam* structures designed by SHoP Architects and fabricated for Design Miami 2016, a different structural logic – a lattice-based structure 3D-printed using Branch Technology's Cellular Fabrication™ freeform process – needs to be employed.

These considerations also have significant implications for 3D printing in terms of cost. The simple logic of how a relatively small increase in dimensions can lead to an exponential increase in volume and weight – and therefore also cost – has a particular consequence for a process that all too often relies on expensive materials, since cost of materials is based on weight. Labour and equipment costs might also mitigate against the overall costs of 3D printing. It might well be that eventually explorations in the use of cheaper materials by practices such as Rael San Fratello (see pp 92–7), and the increasing popularity of 3D printing, help to bring these down. For the moment, however, cost of materials remains a significant limiting constraint, especially when objects become exponentially more expensive to print as size increases.

There are other factors too that limit the size of 3D-printed objects. An obvious constraint is the bed size of a 3D printer. There are notable exceptions, such as the Cellular Fabrication technology employed for the *Flotsam & Jetsam* structures, where the use of gantries and robotic arms extend the range of the printing heads used. And there are also techniques for printing an object in folded form, and then unfolding it after the printing process, as Nervous System has shown (see pp 48–57). However, most 3D-printing technologies are limited by their modest bed size, while folding processes are often highly complex. Equally, the size of the print run itself needs to be taken into account. 3D printing lends itself primarily to one-off customised production, such as individual shoes tailored for the individual user. For larger print runs it would make more economic sense to employ a mould, as in the production of bricks.

In its current form, 3D printing therefore makes most sense for small-scale, customised production. Whatever architects might dream about, it is clear that at the moment at least, it is less suited to large-scale construction. Moreover, it is particularly appropriate for markets where a degree of financial extravagance is acceptable. Obvious examples are jewellery, wedding cakes and haute-couture fashion items. In short, it is fairly clear that while 3D printing remains so expensive, its greatest potential lies in 1:1 body-scale production. The lesson here is that size matters. ⌂

Notes
1. François Roche, 'I've Heard About (A Flat, Fat, Growing Urban Experiment)', in Neil Leach (ed), ⌂ *Digital Cities*, July/August (no 4), 2009, pp 40–5.
2. Charles and Ray Eames (directors), *Powers of Ten: A Film Dealing with the Powers of Ten and the Relative Size of Things in the Universe*, distributed by IBM, 1977.
3. Maarten Schmidt, '3C 273: A Star-like Object with Large Red-shift', *Nature*, 197 (4872), 1963, p 1040.
4. Bill Carithers and Paul Grannis, 'Discovery of the Top Quark', *SLAC Beam Line*, 25 (3), 1995, pp 4–16; Erwin Müller *et al*, 'The Atom Probe Field Ion Microscope', *Review of Scientific Instruments*, 39 (1), 1968, pp 83–6.
5. Jonathan Swift, *Travels into Several Remote Nations of the World, in Four Parts. By Lemuel Gulliver, First a Surgeon, and then a Captain of Several Ships*, Benjamin Motte (London), 1726; Lewis Carroll (Reverend Charles Dobson), *Alice's Adventures in Wonderland*, Macmillan (London), 1865; Merian C Cooper and Ernest B Schoedsack (directors), *King Kong*, distributed by RKO Pictures, 1933; Peter Jackson (director), *King Kong*, distributed by Universal Pictures, 2005; Ishiro Honda (director), *Godzilla*, distributed by Toho, 1954; Joe Johnson (director), *Honey, I Shrunk the Kids*, distributed by Walt Disney Pictures, 1989; Jordan Vogt-Roberts (director), *Kong: Skull Island*, distributed by Warner Brothers Pictures, 2017.
6. For a more detailed discussion, see Knut Schmidt-Nielsen, *Scaling: Why is Animal Size so Important?*, Cambridge University Press (Cambridge), 1984.
7. 'Time Passes More Slowly for Flies, Study Finds', *The Guardian*, 16 September 2013: www.theguardian.com/science/2013/sep/16/time-passes-slowly-flies-study.
8. Michael Fowler, 'Galileo: Scaling' (lecture notes), 2004: http://galileo.phys.virginia.edu/classes/609.ral5q.fall04/LecturePDF/L14-GALILEOSCALING.pdf.
9. For an overview on the height limit for tall buildings, see Nate Berg, 'Is There a Limit to How Tall Buildings Can Get?', Atlantic CityLab, 16 August 2012: www.citylab.com/design/2012/08/there-limit-how-tall-buildings-can-get/2963/.
10. Manuel DeLanda, 'Space: Extensive and Intensive, Actual and Virtual', in Ian Buchanan and Gregg Lambert (eds), *Deleuze and Space*, Edinburgh University Press (Edinburgh), 2005, p 80; Gilles Deleuze, *Difference and Repetition*, Columbia University Press (New York), 1994, p 222.

LACE by Jenny Wu, Tangens necklace, 2014

The design combines three layers of interlocking, self-similar modules that are scaled in size and rotated incrementally from the front to the back of the necklace to give a subtle, perceptual difference as well as working with the contour of the wearer's lower neck and shoulders. The final necklace is printed using SLS technology in an elastic nylon. Jenny Wu trained as an architect and is cofounder (with Dwayne Oyler) of architectural practice Oyler Wu Collaborative.

Behnaz Farahi,
Bodyscape,
2017

This 3D-printed outfit explores the potential of using Langer lines in order to generate a flexible structure which moves and lights up based on the logic of the human body.

MATE
BEHAVI
3D−PR
FASHION

RIAL
OURS IN
INTED
ITEMS

New advances in material technologies and 3D printing are giving a whole new definition to the notion of tailoring. Recent projects by Guest-Editor **Behnaz Farahi** have developed items of apparel that are not only a perfect fit for the wearer, but also interact with his or her surroundings with dynamic qualities. Here she describes their production and their unique functionalities – from bending or bristling in reaction to the onlooker's gaze or the wearer's brain activity, to producing light patterns in response to the body's movement.

Behnaz Farahi,
Caress of the Gaze,
2015

Details of form and material composition of *Caress of the Gaze* printed using Objet500™ Connex™ 3D printer.

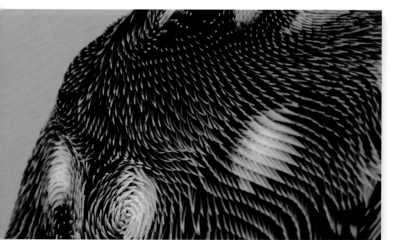

3D printing has opened up the possibility of designing fashion items perfectly tailored to the form of the human body using scanning technologies. However, one of the challenges still remaining is how to fabricate items that can bend and move with the same degree of flexibility as bodily movement. Recent advances in 3D printing now allow us to print objects with the capacity for dynamic behaviours such as bending, folding and twisting. These behaviours allow us to work with the structure and biomechanics of the body, and consequently to tailor forms that not only perfectly fit the form of the body, but also move in response to underlying forces. Moreover, these developments offer new opportunities for designing interactive compliant textiles, which allow our garments to serve as an interface with the world around us. In other words, we can investigate how dynamic materials can serve as interactive interfaces with the world we occupy.

FORM AND BEHAVIOUR

The projects described here have been developed through a process of experimentation to address form, geometry and interactive behaviour. The main objective has been to look at how 'form' or 'geometry' might serve to control the material, to achieve the desired behaviour so as to reflect the dynamism of the human body. The intention is not to design a conventional mechanical system based on moving parts, such as the chain-mail logic used by Niccolò Casas and Nervous System (see pages 34–9 and 48–57), but rather a compliant system in which motion can be achieved through material behaviours themselves. In technical terms, compliant systems adapt their forms through the deflection of flexible members rather than through joints and hinges. From the perspective of fashion, it could also be argued that textile structures achieve their dynamic behaviour thorough microstructural deflection. This approach to 3D printing therefore has something in common with the fashion industry.

The projects additionally engage with 'interactive' design as a way of controlling behaviours and explore its implementation within the fashion industry. Fashion has always been used to express various social and cultural issues. In itself it is a tool of nonverbal communication which can provide a plethora of information about the wearer. Moreover, recent advances in robotic and sensory technologies have presented new opportunities for the world of fashion. If our garments are able to change their shape and texture in real time through robotic control systems, could they not also express our state of mind in a manner not dissimilar to natural systems?

CARESS OF THE GAZE

Caress of the Gaze is an interactive multi-material 3D-printed garment developed at Autodesk's digital fabrication workshop Pier 9, San Francisco, in 2015. It can detect other people's gaze and respond accordingly with a lifelike behaviour.

Our skin is constantly in motion. It expands, contracts and changes its shape based on various internal and external stimuli including not only temperature and moisture but also feelings such as fear, excitement and anger. But what if our clothing could itself behave as an artificial 'skin' capable of changing its shape and operating as an interface with the world, so as to express various social issues such as intimacy, gender and personal identities?

This project offers a vision of the future by investigating the possibility of a second skin fabricated using multi-material 3D printing. It demonstrates how the very latest and most advanced

3D-printing technologies might contribute to the realm of fashion, by exploring the tectonic properties of the materials printed using an Objet500™ Connex™ 3D printer. This technology allows the fabrication of composite materials with varying flexibilities and densities, and can combine materials in several ways with different material properties, all deposited in a single print run. Inspired by the flexible behaviour of reptile skin and fish scales, *Caress of the Gaze* exhibits different behaviours over different parts of the body ranging from rigid to flexible.

For the design of *Caress of the Gaze*, a cellular mesh, which can hold scale-like quills, has been used. The cellular mesh is able to provide sufficient flexibility to afford a range of desirable dynamic behaviours such as twisting, flexing and bending. In addition, the cellular mesh controls the position of the quills, their overlap and hence also their interactions. Meanwhile, the size of the quills and their respective flexibility/rigidity are essential to control the distribution of forces as well as to give the garment a certain aesthetic expression. A series of experiments were therefore conducted to examine the different ratios of soft and flexible to stiff materials on the scale-like members. While the flexible material (Shore 60 Black in this case – Shore being a gauge of hardness) provides flexibility to the entire structure, the rigid material (VeroWhite in this case) provides structural rigidity. The lessons from these experiments were then applied to the form of the garment, so as to allow it to move, bristle and change its shape based on stimuli from the onlooker's gaze.

The project also looks into the potential of an actuation system, assembled as a form of muscle system using shape-memory alloy (SMA) actuators that informs the motion of the artificial 'skin'.

Finally, it investigates how our clothing might interact with other people as a primary interface. For this purpose an image-sensing camera with a lens of less than 3 millimetres (1/8 inch) diameter, and capable of detecting the gender, age and orientation of the gaze of an onlooker, is positioned underneath the garment's quills. This data is relayed to a Teensy microcontroller on the back of the garment, which actuates and controls a network of SMA wires that govern the behaviour of the garment, so that it responds to the onlooker's gaze.

An interactive multi-material 3D-printed wearable which moves and responds based on the onlooker's gaze.

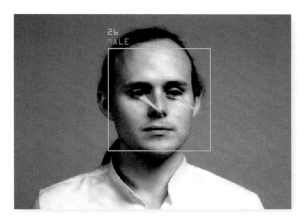

Caress of the Gaze is equipped with a facial tracking camera that detects age, gender and gaze orientation of the onlooker. The compact tracking camera has a lens smaller than 3 millimetres (1/8 inch) diameter and is embedded within the quills.

Study of auxetic behaviours in 3D-printed prototypes with cellular structures using two discrete materials – one soft and one hard. Auxetic structures are ones with a negative Poisson's ratio, which means that they become thicker perpendicular to any pulling force and thinner perpendicular to any pushing force.

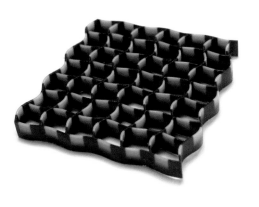

SYNAPSE

Synapse was developed in 2015 at Pier9, San Francisco, and is an interactive multi-material 3D-printed helmet that moves and changes shape based on brain activity. One of the design challenges is to test out the possibilities of using multi-material 3D printing in order to produce a shape-changing structure for the head. As such, the task is to understand the relationship between geometry, material distribution and interactive systems of control. The fabrication process was therefore highly experimental and iterative, with printed samples being continuously tested for their mechanical behaviour.

Similar to *Caress of the Gaze*, this 3D-printed helmet was produced using Objet500 Connex multi-material 3D-printing technology, which is able to print a combination of soft (black) and hard (white, in this case) materials in a single operation.

It is inspired by the system of scaling in fish and reptile skins, which is composed of both stiff and flexible tissues

The design of the helmet aims to provide a flexible/soft structure which enables maximum contraction and expansion. As with *Caress of the Gaze*, it is inspired by the system of scaling in fish and reptile skins, which is composed of both stiff and flexible tissues. However, the material composition of *Synapse* was simplified to a modular elastic mesh which holds rigid, stiff scales in place, to provide maximum curvilinear contraction and expansion.

These principles were then applied to the form of the helmet to create a flexible cocoon around the head, actuated by two small servos, so that it can open, close and change its shape based on stimuli from the brain.

Additionally, the project is an attempt to explore the direct control of the movement of an external object through neural commands from the brain so that we can effectively control the environment around us by our thoughts. The helmet therefore becomes an extension of our bodies. This project aims to challenge the distinction between our bodies and an external object to the point that the differences between them become blurred. The helmet itself is controlled by tracking the brain's behaviour through a NeuroSky™ electroencephalography (EEG) chip and modified Mindflex headset. NeuroSky EEG technology has the ability to assess cognitive load and measure various brainwaves such as Delta (1–3 Hz: sleeping), Theta (4–7 Hz: relaxed, meditative), Low Alpha (8–9 Hz: eyes closed, relaxed), High Alpha (10–12 Hz: daydreaming or consciously practising mindfulness or meditation), Low Beta (13–17 Hz: alert, focused), High Beta (18–30 Hz: busy or anxious thinking and active concentration), Low Gamma (31–40 Hz: multi-sensory processing) and High Gamma (41–50 Hz: conscious perception) values. Additionally, the NeuroSky chip provides proprietary data values related to 'attention' and 'meditation'. In this project, the neural commands related to the 'Attention' level are then translated into actual movement as the visor of the helmet closes or opens up. This operates as a direct interface that allows users to interact with their immediate and non-immediate environments.

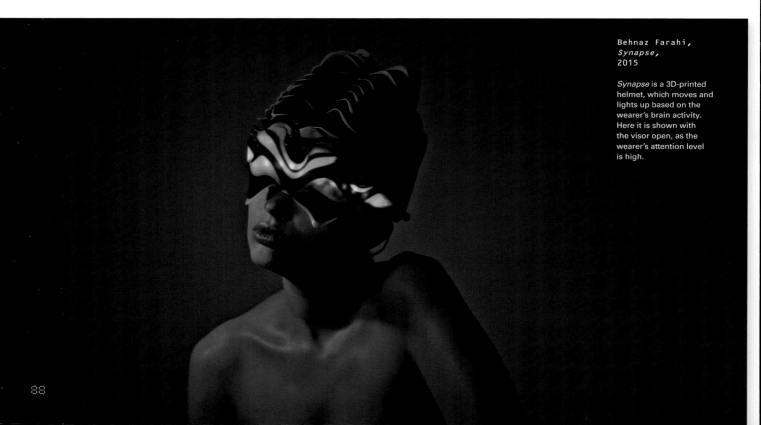

Behnaz Farahi, *Synapse*, 2015

Synapse is a 3D-printed helmet, which moves and lights up based on the wearer's brain activity. Here it is shown with the visor open, as the wearer's attention level is high.

RUFF

While the dynamic behaviour of the two previous projects benefited from the use of advanced multi-material 3D printing, all too often access to this kind of technology is limited. Nonetheless, new findings show that the crucial aspect of the behaviour of 3D-printed materials has to do with their geometrical configuration. As science writer David L Chandler notes, 'The crucial aspect of the new 3-D forms has more to do with their unusual geometrical configuration than with the material itself, which suggests that similar strong, lightweight materials could be made from a variety of materials by creating similar geometric features.'[1]

Ruff was developed in 2015 in Los Angeles, and is a dynamic outfit 3D printed using rigid, fragile materials. *Ruff* takes its name from the protective folded collar popular in Western Europe from the mid-16th to the mid-17th centuries, that is often seen in portraits of the period.

As a collaboration with Dutch fashion designer Pauline van Dongen, this project was an attempt to create a dynamic environment around the body, using 3D-printing technologies. It was a highly hands-on process with printed samples being continuously tested on the body. The main constraint was the challenge of working with ProJet 3500, multi-jet modelling printing technology (MJM), with the availability of rigid and fragile materials.

Interestingly, early tests revealed that structures in the form of a spring proved surprisingly flexible even though they were printed using rigid materials. The design therefore took the form of a folded coil or spiral that could move with the movement of the body. Various topologies and surface modifications were tested in order to enhance the aesthetic expression of the spiralling form, as well as to control the types of motion it could afford around the body. Another constraint was the bed size of the 3D printer, when compared to the scale of the human body. Ingeniously, this issue was solved by twisting the spirals within one another.

Lastly, shape-memory alloy (SMA) spring actuators were incorporated into the design to actuate the contracting or expanding motion of the 3D-printed spiral. This resulted in like–like behaviour, an organic entity that could seemingly crawl over the body.

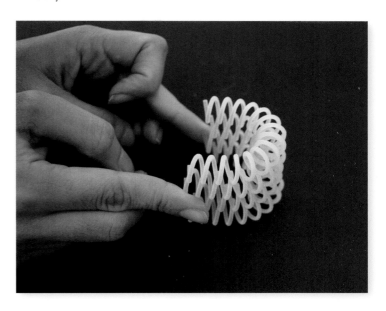

Studies of prototypes printed with rigid, fragile materials using multi-jet modelling (MJM) 3D-printing technology have shown that behaviours can be controlled using very specific geometries. In this case, the spiral forms provide a flexible structure despite the inherent rigidity of the material itself.

Behnaz Farahi and
Pauline van Dongen,
Ruff,
2015

This 3D-printed dynamic outfit moves and crawls around the wearer's body.

Behnaz Farahi,
Bodyscape,
2017

LED strips embedded
underneath the structure
are controlled by a nine-
axis gyroscope and a
small microcontroller.

Interactive lighting systems
have been integrated beneath
the surface in order to enhance
the dynamic performativity
of the wearer's movement.
A small gyroscope capable of
detecting and tracking the nine-
axis shoulder movements of the
wearer sends data to a small
microcontroller that illuminates
two addressable LED strips
placed beneath the surface.

BODYSCAPE

Building upon the knowledge gained in the development of *Ruff*, the aim of *Bodyscape* is twofold. Firstly, *Bodyscape* is an endeavour to explore the role of geometry in creating a dynamic 3D-printed structure for the world of fashion. And, secondly, it is an attempt to create an interactive lighting system so as to amplify the performative qualities of human bodily movement, and to create an enchanting illuminated choreography of the body.

As we have seen in the previous project *Ruff*, spirals, springs and curvilinear forms have greater inherent flexibility. *Bodyscape* draws upon these principles to create a dynamic, flexible outfit despite being printed by using rigid, fragile materials.

A further strategy was to engage with the behaviour and physical properties of human skin. *Bodyscape* is based on the Langer lines of the skin. Langer lines are the topological lines of skin tension, discovered initially in 1861 by the anatomist Karl Langer. These are the lines of least tension that correspond to the natural orientation of collagen fibres in the dermis of the skin, which are generally parallel to the orientation of the underlying muscle fibres. For this reason surgeons use them to determine where to cut the skin during an operation, especially for cosmetic surgery. Most surgeons prefer to make an incision parallel to the Langer lines so that the skin can heal better afterwards, as there is minimum tension between these lines. *Bodyscape* therefore uses both the principles of the spiral as a naturally flexible form and the logic of Langer lines to produce a flexible garment that moves in harmony with the human body.

Finally, interactive lighting systems have been integrated beneath the surface in order to enhance the dynamic performativity of the wearer's movement. A small gyroscope capable of detecting and tracking the nine-axis shoulder movements of the wearer sends data to a small microcontroller that illuminates two addressable LED strips placed beneath the surface. As a result, various lighting patterns emerge according to the forces being exerted by the body as it dances its way through space.

DYNAMIC 3D-PRINTED MATERIALS

These 3D-printed projects address the emerging field of shape-changing structures and interactive systems that bridge the worlds of fashion, art, technology and design. They reveal how 3D-printed wearables can be imbued with responsive and dynamic properties, and endowed with almost lifelike behaviours. Additionally, they exemplify how 3D printing can play an important role in fashion, by augmenting bodily experiences as well as offering new opportunities for clothing to mediate between bodies and their surroundings. They do so in the belief that by implementing design and motion principles inspired by natural systems, we might be able to rethink the relationship between our bodies and the surrounding environment.

One of the important contributions of 3D printing is that it has opened up new approaches to design fields, such as the possibilities of dynamic compliant systems which can be the result of investigations into material properties at both a micro and a macro scale. We can now 3D print incredibly small objects at a 16-micron resolution, which means that in our design process we can engage with the human body at almost the scale of half a red blood cell (approximately 8 microns in width). By defining the material properties at a micro scale, we can also inform their behaviours at a macro scale. Eventually, by taking into account the desired material behaviours, we can design responsive systems that can move and flex not as a result of conventional mechanical systems (such as hinges and joints) but based on their intrinsic material properties.

The notion of such responsive systems, even though they are still at an early stage in their development, could address numerous design challenges and offer the possibility of a radical new approach to clothing, especially considering how 3D-printing technologies are capable of matching the performative qualities of fabrics. ᴆ

Note
1. David L Chandler, 'Researchers Design One of the Strongest, Lightest Materials Known', *MIT News*, 6 January 2017, http://news.mit.edu/2017/3-d-graphene-strongest-lightest-materials-0106.

The notion of such responsive systems could address numerous design challenges and offer the possibility of a radical new approach to clothing

Ronald Rael and Virginia San Fratello

CLAY BODIES

CRAFTING THE FUTURE WITH 3D PRINTING

Emerging Objects
(Ronald Rael and
Virginia San
Fratello),
GCODE.Clay,
2016

The *GCODE.Clay*
body of work includes
hundreds of 3D-printed
vessels that have
unique image maps
and textures on their
surface. G-code is the
computer language
that tells the 3D
printer what to do: it
determines how one
layer of clay is applied
to the next.

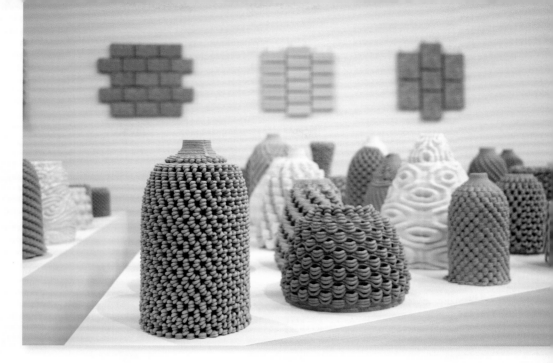

GCODE.Clay explores the possibilities for 3D-printed
clay bodies to function as vases, lamps and tiles.

People have been using clay to make objects and
shelters since time immemorial; but could it also
be a key material of the future? San Francisco-
based 'make-tank' Emerging Objects has been
experimenting with the use of clay in 3D printing,
with sophisticated codes producing woven and
textured forms and mixing different clays together.
The studio's cofounders **Ronald Rael
and Virginia San Fratello** here present
these projects, as well as offering a
potted history of clay's use and nature.
Given its fire-resistance and thermal
qualities, the benefits of eventually
applying such techniques on an
architectural scale are clear.

The swell vase explores possibilities
for light to enter and exit the vessel
through the porosity of the pattern.

Clay is the basic building block of contemporary civilisation. The oldest permanent cities, constructed some 10,000 years ago, were built from unfired mud bricks. Scientists theorise that this humble material also comprises the fundamental building blocks of life itself. One particular type of clay, Montmorillonite, is considered to be the material segue between matter that is not 'alive' and life, which began as a muddy stew of clay and water transformed into living matter by electrical charges from lightning, forming the first microscopic structures that one finds in living cells.[1]

Clay is a combination of alumina, silica and chemically bonded water, and is primarily composed of feldspar, which over the course of millions of years is pulverised through water pressure and transformed into fine particles. Because clay is a product of ubiquitous geological processes, it can be found on every continent, is readily available and inexpensive, and has unique material properties. It exists in a vast spectrum of colours (ranging from white to red to black, with every shade and tint in between); and when fired, it transforms into a stone-like material that lasts indefinitely. In nature, however, clay typically is fairly homogeneous; but when the material is designed, it possesses far more varied characteristics.

The wide range of techniques employed by a potter require clay recipes, which are referred to as a 'clay bodies'. In addition to clay, clay bodies might include silica, grog (pulverised fired ceramic), sand and other materials, which when combined are designed to respond to issues of firing, plasticity, colour, transparency, workability, warping, cracking, shrinkage, porosity, texture, strength and other important factors in the making of ceramics.

EARLY CLAY BODIES

Some of the oldest objects crafted by humankind are made of clay, and the human body is often the subject of these early cultural artefacts. The Venus of Dolní Věstonice is a 26,000-year-old ceramic figurine from the Palaeolithic era discovered in the Moravian basin south of Brno, Czech Republic. This literal clay body was fabricated using local terracotta mixed with powdered mammoth bone. The introduction of bone ash from cattle bones was an innovation also employed tens of thousands of years later, in the invention of bone china in late 18th-century Britain. Not only does the Venus from the Dolní Věstonice site represent the earliest known ceramic technology, she also represents one of the earliest known depictions of the female body and the earliest known use of animal bodies in the making of ceramic objects.[2]

Such clay 'bodies' in the form of torsos or bodies of men, women and animals are also the first objects to have been fired in kilns, which in turn were created by excavating pits of clay from the ground. Interestingly, the Venus figurines (there are well over 200 of them known today[3]) primarily portray a woman's torso only – the head, arms and legs are neglected or absent, and the form of the body is exaggerated. They are voluptuous and often pregnant – a metaphorical representation of the body as a vessel. It was not until over 10,000 years later, around 14,000 BC, that functional ceramic vessels were produced. It was around the same time that architectural ceramic tiles were also invented – the cladding of the vessel of architectural space.

Emerging Objects (Ronald Rael and Virginia San Fratello), *Seed Stitch Wall*, 2016

The *Seed Stitch Wall*'s tiles visually emulate the knitting techniques known as the seed stitch, creating a soft texture – a sweater – for the exterior of a building.

3D PRINTING CLAY BODIES

It is presumed that the first clay vessels were formed by women carrying water, pressing mud into a grass or reed basket in order to make it watertight. Eventually, these baskets were fired in earthen kilns, burning away the grasses, and leaving the ceramic vessel with the impression of basketwork embedded into the surface. Later, the use of woven textiles, such as baskets, became commonplace as a method for making ceramic vessels. Over time, potters pressed textiles into the surface of their clay vessels in order to decorate them, sometimes using cords, notched wheels or other implements to make markings that mechanically replicated the appearance of a textile.[4]

This material and cultural history has inspired the Emerging Objects studio to explore extrusion-based 3D-printing techniques, and has resulted in the development of functional *GCODE.Clay* vessels. Made of 3D-printed layers woven together to make patterns reminiscent of traditional basketry, these recall those first clay pots that were pressed into woven baskets thousands of years ago. The *GCODE.Clay* vessels are made of various clay bodies including B-Mix with grog, a smooth cream-coloured clay body, porcelain, basaltic clay with manganese, recycled clay and local clays.

The woven texture is derived from an exploration into the creative potential of designing with G-code – the programming language for the numerical control of automated machinery. Working directly with the instructions to control a 3D printer, rather than with geometry, a series of controlled deviations are generated that create new expressions in clay defined by the plasticity of the material, gravity, and machine behaviour. Typically, extrusion-based 3D-printed ceramic objects are defined by the layers of clay whose striations are present on the surface of a 3D-printed object. In this case, however, the surface quality takes on the appearance of a textile, with clay being looped, purled and bobbled, as it droops away from the surface. Occasionally there is a dropped 'stitch' which causes a loop to pull away from the surface, making every print unique. The form of the body, or the main section, of the *GCODE.Clay* vessels is voluptuous, swelling towards the centre and resembling a knitted torso. This enlargement allows for a greater volume of water or light to be held within the body of the clay.

The G-code technique is used to examine work at the scale of pottery and at the building scale. The *Seed Stitch Wall* is an exterior cladding system that defines the facade of a small cabin. The 3D-printed ceramic tiles of which it is composed visually emulate the seed-stitch knitting technique often used in outer garments that enclose the human body – although in this case it is used to envelop the architectural vessel.

The tiles and connectors are both 3D printed using fused deposition modelling manufacturing methods. The tiles are printed in clay and the connection system is printed in bioplastic.

Emerging Objects
(Ronald Rael and
Virginia
San Fratello),
Bad Ombrés,
2017

The *Bad Ombrés* body of work
includes 3D-printed vessels
in Cassius Basaltic and Black
Mountain clay in combination
with Polar Ice porcelain.

BAD OMBRÉS

During the third debate of the 2016 United States presidential
election campaign, Donald Trump said he wanted to build a wall
between the United States and Mexico to keep out 'bad *hombres*'.
He was referring to 'bad men' (*hombre* is the Spanish word for
man), but what he said was widely, and satirically, interpreted
(because of his use of a Spanish word in his American accent) as
'bad *ombrés*'. Ombré, which literally translates from the French
as 'shaded', refers to a smooth progression from light to dark.
An ombré allows for unbroken transitions across borders and
between landscapes, very different from Trump's ideas for the
US–Mexico border which he envisions to be defined by a wall.
An ombré, in this case, would be a geopolitical or cultural ombré
that crosses political boundaries fluidly and allows for continuous
cultural connections to be made. In response to Donald Trump's
'bad *hombres*' statement, the Emerging Objects studio has created
a collection of 3D-printed vessels, called *Bad Ombrés*, that
smoothly transition from one material to another. The clay bodies
used in the *Bad Ombrés* collection come from different regions
around the world and are combined in a single tube that extrudes
clay continuously.

The *Bad Ombrés* vessels have colours and tones that merge
into each other, where one clay body is graduated into another,
from light to dark and from translucent to opaque. Black
Mountain and Cassius Basaltic clay, some of the most opaque
and black clays available, transition to Polar Ice porcelain, which
is mined at the Matauri Bay clay pit in New Zealand and is
the world's whitest clay. This unique clay is delicate, resonant
and translucent when struck with light. It is derived from the
alteration of acid volcanic rocks, and the clay body includes
alumina-silicates and plasticisers to make it more workable. The
Black Mountain clay bodies are a combination of fireclays, ball
and red clays that come from pits deep in the southern part of
the United States which are mixed in California to create a newer,
stronger clay body that is easily workable.

Through the use of varying clays, the *Bad Ombrés* are intended
to create new geographic and geologic landscapes – objects that
transcend borders. They are simultaneously rooted in the ground
from which they emerge, yet global and a product of material in
flux. No ombré in this collection will ever be recreated exactly the
same way again. Failure, individuality, distinct character, unique
markings are all what make each object unique – their differences
make them one of a kind, but the transience of material literally
binds them together.

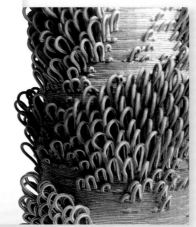

The detail shows how multiple clay bodies are simultaneously
extruded through the nozzle of the 3D printer.

The potterbot at work extruding clay for a *GCODE.Clay* vessel.

The *Bad Ombrés* Purl Stitch Vessel appears tightly woven: it mimics the textures found in traditional pottery into which woven fabrics have been impressed.

The *Bad Ombrés* Loop Stitch Vessel defies gravity and pushes the limits of the material.

FUTURE CLAY BODIES

The *GCODE.Clay* vessels and the *Bad Ombrés* are bodies of work that explore the creation of functional and utilitarian objects which evoke vases, light fixtures and centrepieces. However, they also serve as scale models for proto-3D-printed architecture. It is not difficult to imagine an increase in size. The vessels currently range from 15 to 30 centimetres (6 to 12 inches) in diameter and from 15 to 36 centimetres (6 to 14 inches) tall. The layer height for each coil of clay ranges from 1 to 5 millimetres (0.04 to 0.20 inches). To explore the architectural scale, the Emerging Objects studio is researching and developing a 3D printer that will print a room-size vessel, 2.4 metres (8 feet) wide by 3.7 metres (12 feet) tall, with layer heights varying from 2.5 to 12.7 centimetres (1 to 5 inches) made of local clay extractions.

There are multiple advantages for building with clay in the 21st century. Clay buildings possess thermal mass characteristics that are better than any other material (with the exception of water), which serve as a buffer to exterior temperature fluctuations. A clay building is cool during the day and warm at night because of the delayed release of absorbed solar energy, thus providing a stable and comfortable interior. Clay structures are also fire resistant, and the material is widely available, inexpensive and arguably the most earth-friendly on the planet. Creating an ombré of material technologies that employ traditional knowledge, coupled with 3D printing, produces a highly efficient building system that leaves no waste and is deeply sustainable. Similar to the *GCODE.Clay* vessels, 3D-printed clay architecture will create relief and pattern that contribute to the structural capacity of a clay wall and also serve to be responsive to solar conditions. A textured wall will keep much of its surface in shade in a desert climate, further contributing to cooling the building's interior. Coupled with performative considerations, textured wall surfaces allow for new forms of decoration and customisation, and serve as a way for the building's occupants to establish identity, values and artistic intentions.

Upon their 40th anniversary, the *Smithsonian* magazine announced the 40 most important things they believed one should know about the next 40 years. Number one on their list was that 'Sophisticated Buildings Will Be Made Of Mud'.[5] It is clear that the ecological benefits and sophistication of nearly 30,000 years of material advances in clay, combined with recent developments in additive manufacturing, should not be seen as opposing ends of a technological spectrum, but rather as two paradigms that, when coupled together, have the potential to generate an emergent body of work which will advance the cultural legacy of clay in an era where the machine and the body work hand in hand. ⚿

Notes
1. Cornell University. 'Clay May Have Been Birthplace of Life on Earth, New Study Suggests', *ScienceDaily*, 5 November 2013, www.sciencedaily.com/releases/2013/11/131105132027.htm.
2. Pamela Vandiver *et al.*, 'The Origins of Ceramic Technology at Dolni Vestonice, Czechoslovakia', *Science*, 246 (4933), December 1989, pp 61–2.
3. O Soffer, JM Adovasio and DC Hyland, 'The "Venus" Figurines: Textiles, Basketry, Gender, and Status in the Upper Paleolithic', *Current Anthropology*, 41 (4), August–October 2000, pp 511–37.
4. William H Holmes, 'Use of Textiles in Pottery Making and Embellishment', *American Anthropologist*, New Series, 3 (3), July–September 1901, pp 397-403, http://www.jstor.org/stable/659198.
5. http://microsite.smithsonianmag.com/content/40th-Anniversary/.

Kyle von Hasseln

CRYSTALLINE TECTONICS

AN ARCHITECT'S GUIDE TO 3D-PRINTING SUGAR OR ANYTHING ELSE

Architecture and the culinary arts appear as polar opposites: one generally designed to last, the other inherently ephemeral. But for **Kyle von Hasseln**, a postgraduate architecture research project became the starting point for the two to come together, when he and his partner Liz von Hasseln tried out their second-hand 3D printer with some novel materials. Sugar, chocolate, milk powder, dehydrated powdered fruit: the Los Angeles design firm they cofounded – now known as 3D Systems Culinary Lab – has experimented with them all. Presenting their work, Kyle ponders how it recalls elaborate historical desserts, but with structurally poetic and sometimes challenging twists.

3D Systems
Culinary Lab,
CMYK colour model,
2013

The 200-millimetre (8-inch) centrepiece was digitally colour-mapped and then 3D printed with natural edible dyes in order to understand the subtractive CMYK colour model upon a curved sugar surface.

Among the many mythologies surrounding 3D printing (hereafter: additive manufacturing), a principal misconception continues to uniquely undermine its development – that it can render any material, or nearly any, into any form. This illusion is so thoroughly false it is difficult to succinctly reproach as it wrongfully assumes a uniformity across additive manufacturing technologies where none exists. Additive manufacturing methodologies are as diverse as any other manufacturing class, and each technology, or method of fusion, consequently specialises in certain material classes: laser fusion binds nylon and metals; ultraviolet light hardens photocatalytic epoxy resins; heated plastics may be extruded, crudely, or jetted with precision, and so on. The force of these unique fusing mechanisms conflicts with each material's inherent characteristics (its density, chemical composition and colour) causing the built object to fit and flex, to slip and shear, to anodise and oxidise under the equal pressures of an intense exothermicity and the omnipresence of gravity. Therefore every surface voxel, stepped layer and tortured cantilever of the object traces the inexact struggle of these machine histories, rendering a messy facsimile.

Dear reader, we shall of course let imprecision remain the engineer's lament. We should not hope for perfect replication anyhow. Placing its physical impossibility aside, this would only manifest an object as wholly foreign as an image on a digital screen. As architects we should instead challenge ourselves to recognise the immense opportunity before us. A vast multidisciplinary opportunity that has been left virtually unaddressed by any community because only architects are prepared to reconcile a material with its formal reality in space. Seen in this light, then, additive manufacturing is a gift to architecture as potent and open-ended as a cold, rolled-steel I-beam or a plane of floated glass. Should we choose to negotiate it, it may harken these materials so thoroughly and fundamentally that we may again struggle for a generation to reconcile them before we struggle for another generation to deconstruct them, pausing almost never to express satisfaction. For it is this basic incompatibility that allows architects to ply their virtuosity to the material; to soak and bend the wooden beam, fasten its stoic corners, and all the while revel in the poetics of its structure.

3D Systems
Culinary Lab,
Sugar fish,
2014

The radial gills of this 3D-printed piece reveal a brightly coloured interior. Design precedents included corals and anemones.

LIQUID CRYSTAL DISPLAYS

Additive manufacturing's potential influence is so broad that it encompasses even the culinary arts, a discipline so whimsically unlike architecture that its objects are intentionally (and blissfully) destructed by its clients. Our firm arrived here, like many practitioners, somewhat incidentally. In 2010, in graduate school at the Southern California Institute of Architecture (SCI-Arc), still years before downtown Los Angeles' arts revival, my partner Liz von Hasseln and I procured an antique additive manufacturing ZPrinter with the intention of exploring novel architectural materials such as ceramic, cement and wood powder for an eventual thesis. On a lark, we included salt and sugar in our material audits, for their dreamy translucency as well as for, it must be said, their considerable economic convenience.

Here a curious and seemingly unlikely discovery emerged. Because the ZPrinter works by automating the precise mixture of liquid and dry ingredients, in the case of sugar it therefore began to robotically mimic an ancient manual practice that pastry chefs have relied upon for centuries in order to generate form. Intrinsically, the crystalline mono- and di-saccharide structures of granulated sugar dissolve in the presence of water, but reform, as the aqueous constituent sublimates away, into a newly rigid and structured matrix. This phenomenon is expertly wielded, for example, to construct the ornate calavera skulls used in the Mexican celebration of Día de Muertos (Day of the Dead), which may then be placed onto an altar, as evidence of their symbolic and realised significance, or simply eaten by a child.

In hindsight we often recast breakthroughs as a single epiphanous moment, but I can say that the value of this discovery instead slowly washed into our imaginations over a period of months, rather more like an emergent perspective. Eventually we were forced to acknowledge that this was a rare opportunity to contribute to a nascent field of research. In the summer of 2011 we reluctantly skipped an architectural internship and instead spent our time researching and applying for a US patent for the technology. At SCI-Arc we continued to broaden our research into additive manufacturing by developing a unique photocatalytic technique that was able to generate complex, furniture-scale networked forms far larger than the shallow liquid epoxy basin from which they were drawn. After graduation we opened a design firm in Los Angeles dedicated to exploring the intersection of additive manufacturing and the culinary arts in the context of digital design. Although the firm was quickly acquired by 3D Systems in 2013, it remained under our direction such that the only change was to its name, from The Sugar Lab to 3D Systems Culinary Lab. It soon became exhilaratingly clear, as a constellation of complex material and machine conflicts emerged, that only the architectural mind was set to decipher and reconcile them harmoniously and we were poised to be among this vanguard.

3D Systems Culinary Lab,
Chocolate octahedral lattice,
2013

This 150-millimetre (6-inch) latticework of truncated octahedra was 3D printed with cocoa, sugar and milk powder, and then immersed in a bath of cocoa butter and vanilla.

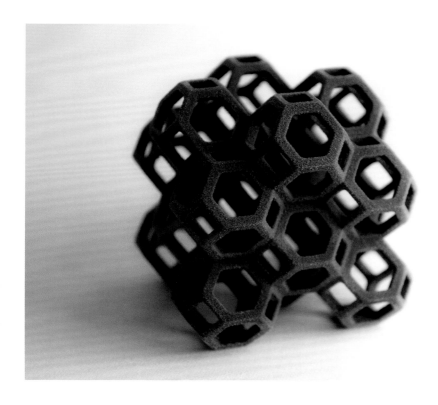

3D Systems Culinary Lab,
Absinthe cocktail,
2014

This absinthe cocktail was built in
collaboration with Modernist Cuisine
for Ferran Adrià. As water dissolves
the Gaudí-inspired 3D-printed sugar
chimney, the drink is sweetened and
diluted in traditional fashion.

A constellation of complex material
and machine conflicts emerged,
that only the architectural mind was
set to decipher and reconcile

3D Systems Culinary Lab,
Geometric candy,
2013

These 25-millimetre (1-inch) geometric
candies were 3D-printed with
dehydrated passion-fruit powder and
sugar with natural colours.

3D Systems Culinary Lab, Porcelain flower, 2013

At 180 millimetres (7 inches) tall, this 3D-printed sugar centrepiece was designed to be evocative of Chinese porcelains imported to Western Europe in the 18th century.

Curving, twisted organic forms were adorned everywhere with hallmarks of mathematics like perfect edges and whole-object symmetry

3D Systems Culinary Lab, Vase, 2012

A network of geometric lace covers thin, vertical ribs arrayed about a curved axis in this 250-millimetre (10-inch) tall 3D-printed vase.

AN IMAGINED PORCELAIN FLOWER

Our first conflict, like architecture's original conflict, was wholly tectonic. Sugar is a mercurial material, and although its inclination to dissolve and re-form is chemically reliable, we found an endless array of outcomes depending on how, where and when water was added. Initially we found that the thickness of an object was critical to its structural success; thicker features stored surplus water that caused problematic warping, whereas thinner features tended to break. In response, we focused on objects primarily built from a single surface of uniform thickness, with compound curvature to maximise strength. We worked and reworked single surfaces until they bent and folded about themselves, gaining unlikely height and negative space. Their raised centres of gravity were counteracted by a prescribed tension between crown and pedestal that bestowed a delicate rigidity throughout.

Keenly aware that our tectonic solution addressed only a part of the formal problem, we further aimed to imbue the memorabilia with a deeper sense of their presence within their own culinary history. Here we sought to balance the seemingly contrary ideals of precision and naturalness. I imagined flowers, grown from porcelain instead of hydrocarbon, like living, breathing ceramic pots that might erupt into geometric blossom. Curving, twisted organic forms were adorned everywhere with hallmarks of mathematics like perfect edges and whole-object symmetry. Such forms were able to negotiate the otherwise stark arrival of digital design, prototyping and automation into the culinary space. They recalled centuries of ornate desserts, but self-evidently achieved remarkable new characteristics that challenged both the chef and the chef's patron to consider them with openness and curiosity.

COMPUTER TO TABLE

Although some of our forms were designed to be too provocative and precious to destroy by conventional dining means, one must also acknowledge the potential for one's own demise. Even here, in what may seem otherwise unthinkable to an architect, we were presented with a subtle avenue for design expression. Because the deconstruction of a food object is often baroquely ritualised, form itself becomes a mechanism to directly influence the ceremony of eating and of celebration. Exercising this profound utility, design can become a force that compels others to adapt to your perspective, and by the means of this conviction you may garner longevity by anointing culture as the guarantor of your idea. ⌂

Design can become a force that compels others to adapt to your perspective

3D Systems Culinary Lab,
Wasabi tartare,
2015

A recipe of dehydrated green and white wasabi, onion, cayenne, garlic and salt, 3D-printed into the form of a hollow quail's egg. The egg is pipetted with quail yolk jam, and cracked open by the diner to complete this wagyu beef tartare.

Zaha Hadid Design
for Georg Jensen,
Lamellae jewellery
collection,
2016

The eight-piece collection
comprises five rings (including
the one shown here that binds
two fingers) and three cuff
bangles, engineered and refined
using 3D-printing design and
manufacturing processes.
Materials include sterling
silver, black rhodium and black
diamonds. The design aims for
an ergonomic tight-fit.

Patrik Schumacher

TECTONISM IN ARCHITECTURE, DESIGN AND FASHION

INNOVATIONS IN DIGITAL FABRICATION AS STYLISTIC DRIVERS

After 'foldism' and 'blobism' comes 'tectonism' – a new branch of the epochal style of parametricism that allows greater expressive and formal variety. It is made possible by an evolving range of digital tools for structural form-finding and physics analysis, linked directly to fabrication. As **Patrik Schumacher**, principal of Zaha Hadid Architects, underlines, these do not remove the need for architects to collaborate with engineers and fabricators, but they do enable them to acquire more reliable intuitions about the logics of these other disciplines. This can only enhance their capacity to produce works that successfully combine communication and social functionality with technical integrity.

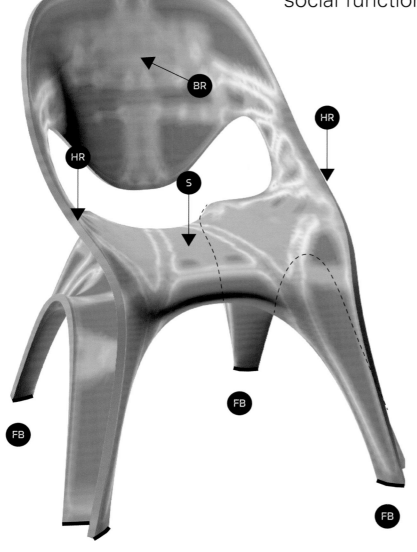

Recent advances in numerically controlled fabrication technologies increasingly feed back into the formal repertoires prevalent in avant-garde architectural, product and fashion design. This feedback is actively and strategically pursued by current protagonists of parametricism, not so much to empower their prior design intentions, but to discover new sensibilities in the rather particular sets of affordances and constraints that come with the different technologies explored.

On the basis of industrial robots as generic fabrication infrastructure, the specific technologies explored are developed within the experimental architectural studios themselves – mostly within and around schools of architecture – rather than being delivered ready-made from outside. While the manifest explicit agenda is the rational utilisation of new productivity-enhancing technologies – where designers are manifestly invested in technical functionality – the latent, implicit agenda is the expansion of architecture's design repertoire and morphology. The pragmatic promise of fabrication efficiency is an attractive premise for designers, but not the most important motivation here: what attracts designers to these technologies is their promise of new creative and expressive powers.

We indeed witness an intense new investment in architecture's stylistic resources. We are witnessing the formation of a new style: tectonism.

FROM ENGINEERING TO STYLE

Tectonism implies the stylistic heightening of engineering- and fabrication-based form-finding and optimisation processes. However, this style does not spell a departure from parametricism. Rather, tectonism is currently the most prevalent and promising 'subsidiary style' (sub-style) within the overarching paradigm and epochal style of parametricism. In retrospect we might distinguish tectonism from earlier phases of parametricism such as 'foldism' and 'blobism'. These older sub-styles are still practised, just as during the era of Modernism the earlier white Bauhaus style continued in parallel with the later Brutalism.

In contrast to these earlier sub-styles, tectonism is embedding a series of technical rationalities that secure both greater efficiency as well as greater morphological rigour, while maintaining sufficient degrees of design freedom to address programmatic and contextual contingencies. Since the principles it utilises are inherently plural and open ended, this additional rigour comes along with additional tectonic variety, and thereby offers a new reservoir of morphological physiognomies. This empowers designers to give a unique, recognisable identity to individual projects. Tectonism delivers much more expressive variety than foldism or blobism, without descending into arbitrary form invention.

While the overarching general design agenda remains parametricism's pursuit of adaptive versatility and complexity, tectonism pursues these with a much richer set of parametric drivers and constraints than earlier versions of parametricism. These drivers originate in sophisticated computationally empowered engineering logics that are now available to architects at early design stages via structural form-finding tools such as RhinoVAULT (for complex compression-only shells) and physics engines like Kangaroo for Grasshopper (to approximate shell or tensile structures), via analytic tools including Principle Stress Lines analysis in Karamba that can also be turned generative, and structural topology optimisation (available in Millipede). Various fabrication- and materially based geometry constraints can also be embedded in generative design

Zaha Hadid Architects Computational
Design Group (ZHA CODE),
3D-Printed Chair,
2014

opposite and below: The design exploits the nearly limitless geometric complexity and fineness of manufacture afforded by high-resolution 3D-printing technologies. It emerged from several successive optimisation processes. After the outer edge line was modelled, the surface was generated via mesh relaxation with Kangaroo. This surface was then the input for a structural topology optimisation to generate a pattern of reinforcement lines via iterative subtraction.

Tectonism implies the stylistic heightening of engineering- and fabrication-based form-finding

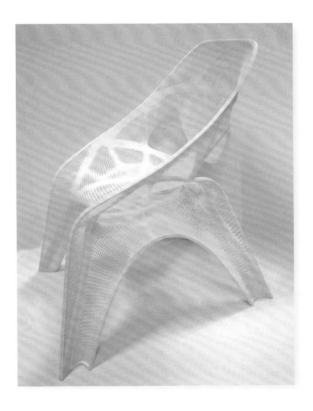

processes that are then set free to search the characteristic solution space delimited by the constraints. The Zaha Hadid Architects Computational Design Group (ZHA CODE) is currently developing many of its own custom tools to model the particular constraints of particular fabrication processes.

All this leads to uniquely characteristic morphologies and features that nevertheless all remain recognisable as variants of tectonism and indeed parametricism because all these techniques follow the methodology of parametricism favouring parametric malleability. In earlier writings I had identified Frei Otto as the only true precursor of parametricism. This identification and honour also applies in relation to tectonism: Frei Otto and the legacy of his research institute are a huge inspiration to its protagonists.

Tectonism delivers both new technical rationalities and articulatory riches that emerge from probing attempts to invent and utilise emerging forms of robotic manufacturing, including robotic 3D printing. It is important to note that tectonism, like the earlier stages within parametricism's development – is already operating across the various design disciplines, although architecture remains its heartland.

Many of the best current protagonists of parametricism might be classified as belonging to tectonism as defined here, including architects Achim Menges, Marc Fornes, Gramazio/ Kohler, Philippe Block and Mark Burry, all of who were featured in the recent *Parametricism 2.0* issue of Δ.[1] Such a classification does not necessarily require self-identification by the protagonists themselves, some of whom might remain sceptical with respect to the very concept of style(s) and might resist being subsumed under any classification. Some of the recent work of Zaha Hadid Architects where structural and environmental engineering logics as well as fabrication logics play an increasingly formative role in the morphology and tectonic articulation of the design can also be classified as tectonism. In particular, the various experimental installations developed within ZHA CODE belong to tectonism, but also buildings such as the Serpentine Sackler Gallery (London, 2013), the 1000 Museum residential tower (Miami, due for completion in 2020), the recently completed King Abdullah Petroleum Studies and Research Center (Riyadh, 2017), as well as various projects in planning at the moment: projects using reticulated concrete shells, tensile structures, exoskeletons, articulated timber structures and so on. Further we can include some of Nike's best products like their Flyknit shoes or some of Odlo's sportswear. Here, fabric tailoring and unusual knitting textures are driven by engineering concerns such as temperature, moisture and movement management via various directions and degrees of elasticity, with gradient ribbing and perforation patterns. These innovations and their aesthetic expression inspired my own forays into fashion design.

For the 2016 exhibition 'Meta-Utopia – Between Process and Poetry' at the Zaha Hadid Design Gallery in London, ZHA displayed a diverse range of experiments in robotic fabrication, including large-scale multi-material 3D printing, robotic plastic extrusion capable of printing lines into space without moulds, concrete printing, robotic component assembly, robotic hot-wire cutting, as well as robotic curved folding of sheet materials. Each of these fabrication techniques imprints its unique, unmistakeable character onto its products, including the shape-range of the overall form as well as the materiality and texture. This means that the concept of 'faktura' is alive and well in our era of robotics. Faktura is the visual trace of the fabrication process in an artefact or work

Patrick Schumacher with Vasilija Zivanic,
Parametric Dinner Jacket,
2013

The jacket is made from neoprene fabric, which is super-light, warm and elastic. The elasticity allows the tailoring to follow the body shape closely without compromising movement and comfort. Zips substitute for buttons everywhere. Laser-cut perforation patterns allow for ventilation where needed, and also enhance the elasticity, as well as delivering an additional substrate for ornamental/semiological expression. The idea is to offer an elegant formal evening jacket perfect for going jogging right after the event.

The concept of 'faktura' is alive and well in our era of robotics

Each of these fabrication techniques imprints its unique, unmistakeable character onto its products, including the shape-range of the overall form as well as the materiality and texture.

of art. The concept emerged in the context of Russian avant-garde art and design during the early Soviet Union, and is seen as giving character to the product.

This new diversity of form making potentials and aesthetic expressions affords a welcome expansion of parametricism's repertoire beyond the smooth non-uniform rational basis spline (NURBS) surfaces that had previously been prevalent. This fuels both programmatic invention as well as semiological articulation. According to my theory of architectural autopoiesis,[2] new styles manifest both new formal concepts as well as a new conception of programme or social function, both connected with the opportunities offered by new technologies.

As Lei Zheng, the curator of the 'Meta-Utopia' show, noted in the catalogue: 'New aesthetic sensibilities are here as much tested as are technological feasibilities, rendering a possible future viscerally tangible, and querying its desirability.' These works query 'technological, aesthetic and anthropological innovations. Fabrication technology experimentation becomes here an engine of both spatio-formal invention as well as socio-programmatic invention.'[3]

While many current design experiments focus on exploring new technologies and architects/designers are inevitably drawn into engineering problematics and thus become proto-engineers, stirring and steering real engineers to come on board, it is important to keep track of the fundamental difference between the design (including architecture) and engineering disciplines. The demarcation between design and engineering is based on the distinction of the social functioning of the built environment from its technical functioning. The clear demarcation of competencies and responsibilities is the more important the closer the collaboration must become with respect to the complex ambitions we pursue in our built environments. While the technical functioning considers the physical integrity, constructability and physical performance of a building, architecture and design must take into consideration that its social function – to order social processes – succeeds via visual legibility. The core competency of architecture/design is thus the task of articulation. However, according to the style and thesis of tectonism, it is new engineering and fabrication logics that deliver the expressive repertoire of articulation to architecture and design. This double burdening of form selection – where technical and communicative performance must be considered simultaneously – becomes possible only due to the expansive proliferation of technically viable options so that an additional selection criterion that composes an orchestrated subset of all technically feasible forms according to compositional/legibility concerns can be accommodated.

Fabrication technology experimentation becomes here an engine of both spatio-formal invention as well as socio-programmatic invention

Zaha Hadid Design and Ai Build,
Puddle Chair,
2017

The chair was designed specifically to be manufactured via freeform, multicolour (black and blue) robotic 3D printing. The sofa's space-frame is optimised for lightness, material robustness and structural integrity, and its intricate design is layered with an artificial cloth to transform it into a comfortable seating surface with a stimulating ripple texture.

ZHA CODE,
Cirratus 3D-printed concrete vase,
2017

The design is an interpretation of a classic vase by architect Alvar Aalto. A bespoke algorithm produces complex double-curvature geometry that adheres to and exploits the specific constraints of concrete printing manufacturing and expresses the additive, layer-by-layer process of its making.

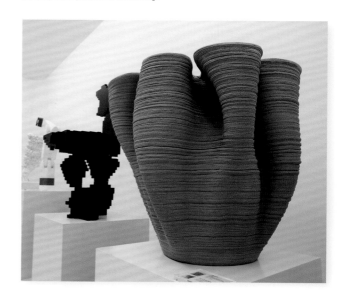

TECTONIC ARTICULATION

The relationship between the technical and communicative dimensions of the built environment leads to the concept of tectonics, or more precisely 'tectonic articulation',[4] here understood as the architectural selection and utilisation of technically motivated, engineered forms and details for the sake of a legibility that aims at an information-rich, communicative spatial morphology, for the sake of visual or tactile communication.

It was the Guest-Editor of this issue of *AD*, Neil Leach, who first used the concept of tectonics in connection with the digitally based design movement I later termed parametricism, in his 2002 anthology entitled *Designing for a Digital World*,[5] and then in a follow-up work entitled *Digital Tectonics* (2004).[6] According to Leach, the title was intended as a strategic reappropriation of the term 'tectonics' from the more conservative – and seemingly moralising – way that Kenneth Frampton had used it in his earlier *Studies in Tectonic Culture* (1995).[7] I welcome this general reappropriation as a basis for my much more specific concept of tectonics that implies the capacity (if not always the explicit agenda) of communication.

The concept of tectonic articulation applies to all design disciplines from architecture to product design and fashion, and so does the distinction between design and engineering implied in the distinction between technical and social functionality. Within our complex information/network society, the built environment and the world of artefacts have to share the task of information processing and communication: they become an important source of information helping us to navigate and orient within our increasingly complex social world. Thus the social functionality of a designed space or artefact crucially depends on its communicative capacity. All design – across all design disciplines – is to an important extent communication design. In fashion design this is often more obvious than in architecture or product design, but it applies universally across all design disciplines. The designed environment together with the world of designed artefacts – effectively the totality of the phenomenal world that surrounds us – functions as an interface of communication. This also includes graphic and web design. Therefore all human interactions, whether face-to-face or mediated, depend on being framed and facilitated by designed spaces and artefacts that should take this crucial function into account.

The history of architecture abounds with examples where architectural elements and features with technical functions become the object of articulatory or 'ornamental' endeavours. However, we need to understand the instrumentality of ornament. We need to grasp ornament not in contrast to performance, but as a special type of communicative performance. A technically efficient morphology might thus also assume an articulatory, communicative function. The articulatory integration of the morphological consequences of technical requirements is always the more elegant solution than the attempt to fight and deny them by covering them up with a separate communicative surface. This latter stance would require the invention of additional communicative features because social distinctions desire and require expression. However, the utilisation of the initially technically motivated morphological features for the characterisation of spaces is not only more economical, but leads to a higher level of credibility of the communication because the morphological feature that is now to become a signifier is often already an index of the intended meaning rather than a merely arbitrary symbol.

In the terminology of the founder of semiotics, Charles S Peirce, tectonic articulation thus transforms 'indexical signs' into 'symbolic signs'.[8] This process too gives degrees of freedom to the designer in the selection of the indexical features that might be heightened and systematised to become elements of a semiological system of signification. To pursue tectonic articulation, architects need to guide and orchestrate the engineering investigations and then select the engineering options that most suit their primary task, namely to fulfil the posed social functions via spatio-morphological communications. The adaptive differentiation of loadbearing structures as well as the adaptive differentiation of volumes and envelopes according to the building's environmental performance (with respect to its exposure to sun, wind, rain and so on) as well as differentiations that stem from fabrication logics (tessellations, tool-path patterns) afford many opportunities for differential tectonic articulation. A lawfully differentiated built environment would therefore be much more legible and navigable than Modernism's mute, isotropic order of repetition or the visual chaos of postmodernist collage.

The development of sophisticated computational design tools within both the architecture and engineering disciplines, and within the construction industry, means that the scope for nuanced tectonic articulation has much increased. The realisation of this potential requires an intensified collaboration between innovative architects, engineers and fabricators. Although there can be no doubt that architecture remains a discourse that is distinct from engineering and construction, close collaboration with these disciplines as well as the acquisition of reliable intuitions about their respective logics are increasingly important conditions for the design of contemporary high-performance built environments. These intuitions can be more reliably acquired if architects and designers engage in amateur proto-engineering by using the various physics engines cited above to experiment with fabrication processes. Tectonism is committed to such practises that demand additional skills and knowledge, and that deliver a new, rich formal repertoire of articulation. These new articulatory powers can be employed in a design agenda of communication made explicit: design is communication. *AD*

Notes
1. See Patrik Schumacher, *AD Parametricism 2.0: Rethinking Architecture's Agenda for the 21st Century*, March/April (no 2), 2016.
2. Patrik Schumacher, *The Autopoiesis of Architecture*, Volumes 1 and 2, John Wiley & Sons, 2010 and 2012.
3. Lei Zheng, *Meta Utopia: Between Process and Poetry*, 'Meta-Utopia' exhibition catalogue, Zaha Hadid Design Gallery, London, 2017, p 2.
4. This concept of 'tectonic articulation', defined with reference to semiology, was first introduced by the author in 'Tectonics: The Differentiation and Collaboration of Architecture and Engineering', in Ursula Kleefisch-Jobst et al, *Stefan Polonyi: Bearing Lines–Bearing Surfaces*, Edition Axel Menges (Stuttgart and London), 2012.
5. Neil Leach (ed), *Designing for a Digital World*, John Wiley & Sons (Chichester), 2002.
6. Neil Leach, David Turnbull and Chris Williams (eds), *Digital Tectonics*, John Wiley & Sons (Chichester), 2004.
7. Kenneth Frampton, *Studies in Tectonic Culture*, MIT Press (Cambridge, MA), 1995.
8. Charles S Peirce, 'What is a Sign?', *The Essential Peirce: Selected Philosophical Writings 1893–1913*, Indiana University Press (Bloomington, IN), 1998.

SHAPE

Madeline Gannon

Madeline Gannon/ATONATON,
Tactum,
2014

Tactum strikes a balance between skin-centric gestures and intelligent geometry when integrating mechanical or functional elements of a design. For this watch band, the clips for the watch face are topologically defined within the design's parametric model. While the designer is focusing on the form of the design, the CAD backend places and regenerates these mechanically precise, low-tolerance geometries.

THE OF TOUCH

ON-BODY INTERFACES FOR DIGITAL DESIGN AND FABRICATION

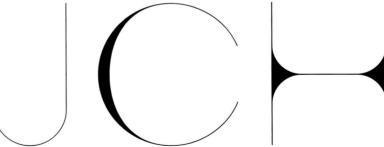

Like a building to its site, true body architecture must be properly fitted to the specific topography of the wearer's body. Reverb and Tactum are two digital modelling tools developed by Pittsburgh-based research studio ATONATON for this very purpose. Using projection mapping, depth sensing and gesture recognition, they allow users to physically interact with a virtual design process that links directly through to a 3D-printed output. **Madeline Gannon**, the studio's leader, explains how they work.

Although designers are finding increasingly innovative ways for 3D-printed artefacts to adorn and augment our bodies, the digital tools for crafting such imaginative creations are fairly limited. Computer-aided design (CAD) systems were created to design buildings, boats, cars and planes – not things for the body. Digital design for the body brings inherently different challenges: not only are the complex curves and non-Euclidean contours of the body ill-suited for conventional 3D modelling tools, but every *body* is different. Creating variations of a design for multiple body types can be a laborious task with current CAD systems. For digital tools to better support body-centric design, they require new ways to directly reference and engage the body.

Our bodies are continuously broadcasting information to the surrounding environment. A person's body language, posture, hand gestures and proximity to others communicate a wealth of data about the individual's internal state of mind and intentions. The work of the ATONATON research studio based in Pittsburgh, Pennsylvania, explores how these spatial transmissions can be captured, recognised and translated into actionable information for digital design tools. The body itself is a far more dynamic interface than any conventional CAD environment, and the following immersive system developed by ATONATON demonstrates how it can be transformed into an interactive canvas for digital design and fabrication.

REVERB: CONTEXT-AWARE FABRICATION
Reverb is a fabrication-aware design tool that translates real-world hand gestures into intricate geometries that can be immediately printed and worn on the body.[1] First, it uses a depth sensor to capture and import a 3D scan of the designer's body into its virtual environment. This same depth sensor is then used to recognise and track the designer's mid-air hand gestures, allowing them to reach into the computer and use their own hands to interact with a semi-autonomous geometry living inside Reverb. To begin crafting a digital design, the designer moves their hand closer towards the 3D-scanned body: the intelligent geometry inside Reverb becomes attracted to the hand, and the system records the mesh of this base module as it is manipulated through space and time. As the designer's hand continues to influence and guide the geometry through the virtual environment, these intuitive gestures result in complex lattice structures sculpted around their digitised body.

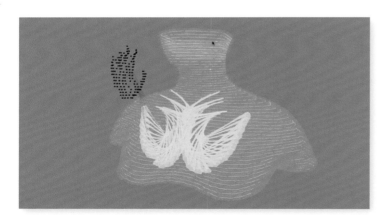

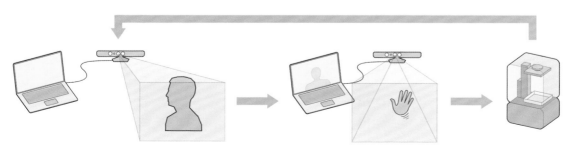

**Madeline Gannon/ATONATON,
Reverb,
2013**

opposite left: Reverb is a context-aware 3D-modelling environment that lets you design ready-to-print wearables around your own body. The screen grab here shows the designer's digitised hand draping an intricate, latticed design around a 3D scan of her body.

opposite bottom: Reverb's three-phase workflow allows the designer to move fluidly between 3D scanning, 3D modelling and 3D printing a wearable artefact. Unlike conventional CAD software, every Reverb design is crafted around an intelligent context – the digitised body — and is therefore inherently sized to fit its owner.

sequence right: The collar on the top has a medium density of lattice modules that allows it to be stretched when placing around a person's neck. The collar in the centre has a low density of modules that accentuate the torsion forces it receives when resting on the shoulders. The collar to the bottom is printed from a rubber-like elastomer; it has the highest density of modules, which absorbs and diffuses light in a dramatic fashion.

below: Wearable artefacts generated through Reverb show traces of their anatomical beginnings. Although these baroque designs may seem quite foreign to the body, they illustrate a deep contextual awareness in the way they delicately meet the nape of the neck, the curve of the shoulder or slope of the bust.

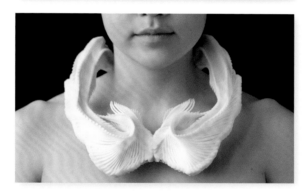

The designer's expressive yet imprecise hand gestures can drape intricate digital forms that fit precisely around a physical body.

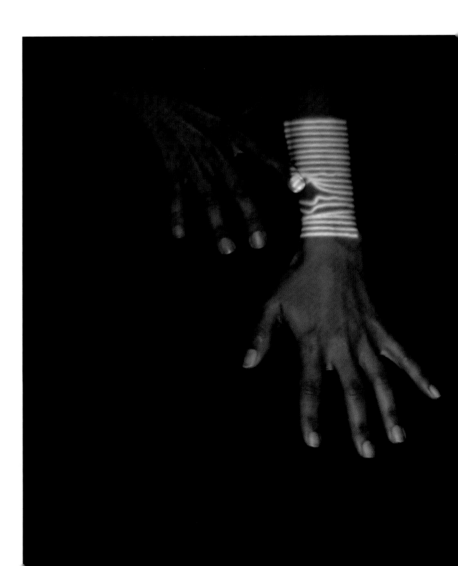

Madeline Gannon/ATONATON,
Tactum,
2014

above: Tactum uses depth sensing and projection mapping to detect and display touch gestures on the skin. The sequence here shows the process of designing a bracelet: a designer pokes and pinches the interactive geometry into a desired form (left), then closes their fist to freeze the design (middle). Once they re-open their hand, the digital design is exported to be printed and worn back on the body (right).

right: Touch gestures detected through Tactum transform a projected design into a ready-to-print, ready-to-wear piece of jewellery.

Gestural interfaces can provide an intuitive means for interacting with digital geometry. However, there is a trade-off: the more natural the interface, the less precision and control we have over the final form. By contrast, Reverb uses physics-based modelling to strike a balance between intuitive interaction and intricate geometry. Its base geometry is built from a spring skeleton that preserves the module's geometric and physical attributes, no matter how it is manipulated by a designer's hand. Moreover, the 3D scan is embedded with an opposing particle system that repels the base module and prevents intersections with the digitised body. As a result, the designer's expressive yet imprecise hand gestures can drape intricate digital forms that fit precisely around a physical body.

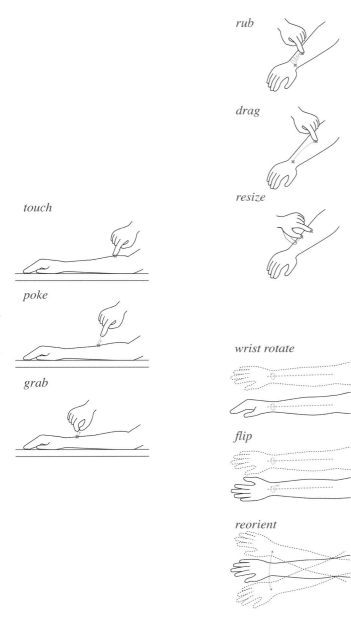

Tactum can detect and track nine unique skin-centric gestures using only one above-mounted sensor.

TACTUM: ON-BODY DESIGN

Tactum is an augmented modelling tool that allows 3D-printed wearables to be designed directly on to the body.[2] The system uses a single depth sensor to detect a user's tactile interactions with their skin. Once detected, these skin-centric gestures are used to stimulate interactive, fabrication-aware geometry that is projected on the body. This allows a designer to quickly iterate on a wearable design, at a 1:1 scale and in situ, just by poking, rubbing or pinching the projected geometry on his or her skin. Once a desired form is achieved, the designer closes his or her hand to export the design for 3D printing.

Unlike traditional 3D-modelling environments, Tactum only allows ready-to-print, ready-to-wear designs to be generated. The interactive geometry inside Tactum is built from distinct features extracted from the arm: the same sensor that detects skin-centric gestures also tracks and segments the wrist, elbow, forearm and hand from the overall arm. Segmentation enables Tactum's interactive geometry to parametrically adapt to many individual bodies, so that the wearables produced are inherently sized to fit the designer. This level of embedded ergonomic intelligence is also necessary for Tactum's projected geometry to remain visually attached to the physical body as it moves around the workspace. Consequently, Tactum demonstrates how designing *for* the body *on* the body can provide a far more fluid, intuitive and facile experience while exploring and experimenting with a wearable design.

EMBODIED INTERACTION

Reverb and Tactum illustrate how new computational techniques can blur the digital–analogue boundary when making things for the body. Augmenting digital workflows with depth sensors and gesture recognition enables these interfaces to come out of the computer and directly engage the body. Moreover, many of the technical challenges designers face in creating 3D-printed wearables are mitigated when design tools are embodied with a more contextual understanding of how they are being used. The experimental interfaces presented here show how more fluid and intuitive means to communicate with digital design tools can augment and enhance our creative capabilities. As new techniques for combining digital technologies with the physical world continue to advance, the body will persist as a complex and exciting context for the future of digital design. ⌂

Notes
1. See Madeline Gannon, Tovi Grossman and George Fitzmaurice, 'Tactum: A Skin-Centric Approach to Digital Design and Fabrication', in *Proceedings of the 33rd Annual ACM Conference on Human Factors in Computing Systems* (CHI '15). ACM, New York, 2015, pp 1779–88.
2. See Madeline Gannon, 'Reverberating Across the Divide: Bridging Virtual and Physical Contexts in Digital Design and Fabrication', in *Proceedings of the 34th Annual Conference of the Association for Computer Aided Design in Architecture* (ACADIA), Los Angeles, 2014, pp 357–64.

Eric Goldemberg

THE SONIC SPECTACLE OF THE ENHANCED BODY

MONAD Studio
(Eric Goldemberg and
Veronica Zalcberg),
Anouk Wipprecht and
Viktoria Modesta,
SONIFICA: Turning
the Body into
an Instrument,
2016

this page and previous spread:
The sonic bustier was
customised to shape its fluid
architectural components around
the performer's specific
postures, allowing for the
necessary freedom of movement
and enhancing the capacities of
the body.

Florida design practice MONAD Studio's focus is rhythmic affect at all scales. Having already experimented with 3D-printed musical instruments, they embarked upon SONIFICA: a collaboration with interaction designer Anouk Wipprecht and the world's first 'bionic' pop singer, Viktoria Modesta. Sensors and actuators in a sonic bustier, and an integrated accelerometer in a prosthetic leg, transform Modesta into a living musical instrument. MONAD Studio cofounder **Eric Goldemberg** outlines how this was achieved and argues that it is reflective of a new mode of expression, defined and driven by transdisciplinarity.

SONIFICA: Turning the Body into an Instrument represents a new type of sonic spectacle where the architecture of the body is enhanced with 3D-printed devices that augment the performer's capacity. The experimental integration of architecture and music by means of advanced 3D modelling and digital fabrication technologies unlocks new potentials for innovative artistic performances, where collaboration between different disciplines applied to the scale of the human body can generate a leading-edge type of synthetic design assimilation that questions existing models of representation, stretching the limits of architecture by opening it up to the field of spatial-sensorial composition.

The synthesis of aesthetic, functional and spiritual power sparked by architects MONAD Studio with interaction designer Anouk Wipprecht and bionic pop artist Viktoria Modesta in the live performances of SONIFICA throughout 2016 generated a new mode of alliance beyond disciplinary boundaries. Supported by the Florida International University Department of Architecture, the interdisciplinary team was able to find common ground in the sonic world as medium, and the human body as artistic subject, creating new design dimensions geared towards innovative ways of social engagement through sensation, emotion and healing. The fusion of the different capacities of each of the collaborators elevated the challenge to unforeseen organisations of matter that revealed how much can be achieved by entangling our sensibilities and experimenting with spatial perception.

Viktoria Modesta challenges people's perceptions of limiting disabilities and the impact of this on our social status by redesigning possibilities for the body. As an amputee, she has been able to turn her bodily constraint on its head. For the SONIFICA project, her performative capacity was augmented by a 3D-printed sonic bustier designed by MONAD Studio and Anouk Wipprecht with tusks equipped with sensors and actuators that allowed her to modulate sound during live performances. Along with a new prosthetic leg, furnished with an accelerometer, this allowed her to become a living music instrument and to interact both spatially and sonically with an ensemble of musicians playing MONAD Studio's 3D-printed musical instruments. The premiere took place in the Miami Design District, in the atrium of the Moore Building, with Zaha Hadid's Elastika installation as part of the stage set. The project is one of many possible examples of technology and creativity combined with the human will to exceed limitations and produce new meaning, intensifying some fundamental existential questions.

Focusing on how the taxonomy of sound can provoke the senses, for the design of the sonic bustier and prosthetic leg the team began by applying the same methodology used previously by MONAD Studio on its 3D-printed musical instruments, analysing the ergonomic relationship between musicians and their instruments via digital

MONAD Studio
(Eric Goldemberg and
Veronica Zalcberg),
Anouk Wipprecht and
Viktoria Modesta,
SONIFICA: Turning
the Body into
an Instrument,
New World Symphony,
Art Basel,
Miami Beach,
Florida,
2016

Accompanied by two musicians playing MONAD Studio's 3D-printed piezoelectric violins, Viktoria Modesta wore a 3D-printed sonic bustier with tusks equipped with sensors and actuators that allowed her to trigger and modulate pre-programmed sounds input remotely to her tusks via a wireless controller during her live performances. A prosthetic blade leg with interactive lighting completed the ensemble.

Along with a new prosthetic leg, furnished with an accelerometer, this allowed her to become a living music instrument

mapping of their posture during performances. This dynamic re-conception of the prosthetic structure of sonic artefacts based in the movements of the performer laid the foundation for the development of the architecture and emergent aesthetics for Viktoria Modesta's body, seamlessly incorporating Anouk Wipprecht's interactive gadgets into the morphology of the bustier, tusks and leg to generate a novel spectacle. Precise 3D modelling allowed for the optimisation of the points of friction between body and instrument so that new capacities for the production of sound could be engineered using interactive devices and malleable geometries adaptable to the supple topology of the body to establish a new kind of design intelligence. This fusion of sensibilities enabled multiple technical constraints to be incorporated seamlessly as rules that helped to calibrate the design through the various 3D-printed iterations.

The interesting geometries designed as part of this collaborative work were synthetically applied to create a dynamic interplay, where fashion meets architecture and technology. The way the project has evolved represents a more open approach, shaped not by any specific domain or discipline, but rather by a collective impetus that demonstrates a new mode of expression, a new type of art that is inclusive of architecture, design, fashion, engineering, interactivity and sonic performance; where projects emerge according to the combined intent of transdisciplinary sensibility, and not the other way around. ᗐ

MONAD Studio (Eric Goldemberg and Veronica Zalcberg), Anouk Wipprecht and Viktoria Modesta, SONIFICA: Turning the Body into an Instrument, Young Artists Initiative, The Moore Building, Miami, Florida, 2016

above: The exploration of the ergonomics of the human form and the expression of the instrument were particularly evident as the protruding tusks were situated right in front of the musician's hands for an easy grip of the interactive buttons and slider that controlled the sound.

right: In this performance, Viktoria Modesta was supported by an ensemble of five musicians playing 3D-printed musical instruments designed by MONAD Studio (Eric Goldemberg and Veronica Zalcberg) with musician-luthier Scott F Hall.

This tea set for Alessi is one example of architects experimenting with product design, seemingly a scaled-down version of Lynn's architecture. However, architects are increasingly starting to work with digital technologies on a large scale in a new kind of practice that operates across scales.

COUNTERPOINT
06/2017
Nº 250
AD

Gilles Retsin

TEAPOTS, DRESSES AND CHAIRS

Contrary to the impression given throughout this issue of Δ, the future of the architectural profession is not to be found in scaling down to the level of household products and fashion items. So argues London-based architect **Gilles Retsin**, who teaches at the Bartlett School of Architecture. While embracing transdisciplinarity and engagement with multiple scales in architectural practice and education, he sees these as evidence of a more research-based turn, rather than an abandonment of architects' key calling. Although also opening up the profession to a product- rather than service-based business model, small-scale objects essentially offer a context for experimentation with new technology that then begs to be scaled up.

Beaux-Arts Ball, Manhattan, New York, 1931

New York's famous architects dressed up as miniature versions of their skyscrapers for the annual ball. Many 3D-printed fashion items can equally be understood as miniature architecture – scaled-down exercises in formal articulation.

In an academic and writing career that stretches beyond two decades, Neil Leach has a proven track record of provocation. This is apparent in the preface of his 1999 book *The Anaesthetics of Architecture*,[1] where he sets out to deliberately incite in the style of Jean Baudrillard's *Fatal Strategies* (1990),[2] and in more recent writings such as the provokingly titled article 'There is No Such Thing as Digital Architecture' (2015).[3] This issue of △ is no less provocative. In his Introduction, Leach argues that architects with a technological interest had better migrate into fashion and wearables rather than staying in 'a profession struggling to survive' (pp 6–15). The argument then suggests a need to understand 3D-printed fashion and wearables as a form of proto-architecture. Finally, these claims are primarily supported by the assumption that 3D printing is hard to scale. I will assume here that the issue is equally meant as a provocative call to order, asking the digital design community the pertinent question: 'How did we end up in fashion, and how do we get out ?'

This question is especially important today, given that after two decades of successful and prolific experimentation with digital design, the digital turn is now facing some backlash. Since the financial crisis of 2008, events like Alejandro Aravena's 'Reporting from the Front' 2016 Venice Architecture Biennale have given a platform to the criticism that the digitally intelligent architecture of the pre-2008 period was not exactly interested in the social and political realm. In this context, an exit to the fashion world does not seem a particularly convincing argument for the importance of digital design.

COSTUME BALL

Delirious New York (1978) has a famous image of a group of New York architects dressed as their skyscrapers, under which the book's author Rem Koolhaas notes: 'research, disguised as costume ball'.[4] The costumes that Chrysler Building architect William Van Alen and his friends wore are scaled-down architecture, both amusing and uncomfortable at the same time. If they appeared outside of the catwalks, the 3D-printed dresses in this △ would probably be equally amusing and uncomfortable. They represent the language we have come to associate with the last two decades of digital research in architecture: smooth, often biologically inspired, continuously differentiated forms. Not unlike Greg Lynn's Alessi Tea and Coffee Towers (2003), they are almost like miniature buildings – scaled-down architectural strategies. But are these kinds of small-scale experiments really so important for architecture? As Mario Carpo notes: 'A technological revolution heralded by a cohort of ninety-nine teapots is easily disparaged.'[5] Historically, architects have of course been prolific at designing products, and in doing so blurring the boundaries of the discipline. The list is endless, from Art Nouveau architect Henry van de Velde's infamously unwearable fashion pieces to Adolf Loos's set of whiskey glasses (1931).

The rise of new digital fabrication technologies has resurrected this history and produced a new generation of designers who confidently work across multiple scales and disciplines. As this issue of △ successfully points out, these techniques have also enabled new business models for architects. Instead of a traditionally service-oriented approach, architects such as Francis Bitonti, Nervous

XtreeE,
3D-printed tripod surface,
2016

Co-founded by architect Philippe Morel,
XtreeE uses industrial robots to 3D print
large-scale concrete elements for the
building industry. These offer greater
formal freedom, and reduce the need for
expensive manual labour and formwork.

This shift is taking place across scales, and is not at all giving up on architecture

Digital Building Technologies,
3D-printed stay-in-place formwork,
Institute of Technology in Architecture,
ETH Zurich,
2017

Led by Benjamin Dillenburger, the Digital Building Technologies research group is developing a concrete slab that makes use of 3D-printed formwork. The slab is structurally optimised, and integrates technical devices in its complex geometry.

System and Steven Ma have started to experiment with product-based models. Similarly, we see startups emerging that focus on the large scale – Jelle Feringa with Odico, Philippe Morel with XtreeE, and Daghan Cam with Ai Build among them. These firms blur the boundaries between architecture, engineering, product design and software development, and this is also reflected in education. In the MArch Architectural Design and MSc Architectural Computing courses I co-direct with Manuel Jiménez at the Bartlett School of Architecture, University College London (UCL), this cross-disciplinary approach is already prevalent. Students experiment with everything from wearables to chairs, tables, software applets and robots, while eventually ending up with architectural-scale proposals. With a combination of design, making and tech skills, they are equipped to continue their careers in a variety of disciplines, not excluding architectural practice itself.

While this perhaps seems to align well with Leach's vision, there is a crucial difference. I would understand much of the work in this ⌂ as part of a larger turn in architecture towards research, which sees architects developing their own tools, machines, software, products, companies and research facilities. Contrary to Leach, I would argue that this shift is taking place across scales, and is not at all giving up on architecture. Moreover, through its focus on technology, this cross-scalar, research-driven approach is future-proofing architecture for the 21st century. If we want to keep our cities and our discipline out of the hands of IBM, Google and other smart-city advocates, it is better we do not marginalise ourselves by migrating en-masse to the catwalks.

SCALE AND SCALABILITY

It is difficult to argue in 2017 that 3D printing is failing to scale up. In the past five years, architects and researchers have achieved remarkable results with large-scale digital manufacturing. Research institutes are now successfully 3D printing concrete, often in collaboration with industry. XtreeE, for example, 3D prints concrete building elements using industrial robots. These elements have the same strength as traditional concrete, but offer far more formal possibilities and a shorter production chain. At ETH Zurich, Benjamin Dillenburger's Digital Building Technologies group is developing a large 3D-printed floor slab that integrates building services, formwork and structure. His colleagues from the Block Research Group exhibited a structural floor slab in 3D-printed sandstone at the 2016 Venice Biennale.

But it is not only in academic research that large-scale 3D printing is explored: construction company Laing O'Rourke is already using formwork to produce complex concrete panels for Crossrail.[6] Other industry giants, such as LafargeHolcim – the biggest concrete producer in the world – are actively investing and researching concrete 3D printing. The previously mentioned research institutes and companies have started to develop their own machines and workflows that are able to print materials usually used in the construction industry. The processes make building cheaper, by removing the need for expensive manual labour and by simplifying complicated production chains. In this sense, Leach's concerns about scalability do not really hold up. This approach is different to that of most of the architects and designers mentioned in the issue who make use of conventional, commercially available 3D printers. These off-the-shelf printers are indeed expensive and difficult to scale up, and therefore only applicable to the small scale.

131

Hyunchul Kwon, Amreen Kaleel
and Xiaolin Li,
CurVoxels 3D-printed chair,
Bartlett School of Architecture,
University College London (UCL),
2015

To avoid using expensive, conventional 3D printers,
architects have started to develop their own software,
machines and workflows. This new, research-based
architecture has an impact on education. In this case
students from the Bartlett B-Pro Architectural Design
programme turned an industrial robot into a large 3D
printer by adding a custom-made extruder.

Gilles Retsin and Manuel Jiménez,
VoxelChair 1.0,
Design Computation Lab,
Bartlett School of Architecture,
University College London (UCL),
2017

This robotically 3D-printed chair is first and foremost a piece of architectural research, advocating a shift in the digital design paradigm from continuity to discreteness. The chair was assembled out of thousands of serially repeated, discrete tool-path fragments, and then robotically 3D printed in one go.

THE *RED AND BLUE CHAIR*

The experiments coming out of this new research-based architecture are effectively proto-architectural, even though they are most often not on the scale of a building. Just as Gerrit Rietveld's *Red and Blue Chair* (1917) is a prototype for the Rietveld-Schröder House in Utrecht (1924), the chairs and furniture pieces developed as part of the Bartlett MArch and MSc programmes aim to develop knowledge for larger architectural systems. The *Red and Blue Chair* advances a new form of spatial composition; a volume dissolved by lines and planes. This spatial quality then later comes back in the Schröder House, and resonates further in many other Modernist compositions. By using only standardised measures of timber, and stripped of ornamentation, the *Red and Blue Chair* also articulates a new idea of production. Similarly, the Bartlett chairs and furniture pieces address large-scale design issues while investigating new digital production workflows.

The robotically 3D-printed VoxelChair 1.0, for example, investigates a discrete design method. Questioning the paradigm of continuity, as argued for by Greg Lynn in *Animate Form* (1999),[7] the chair looks at an architectural design strategy based on discrete syntax.[8] In a continuous paradigm, its overall shape would be first defined and then sliced into thousands of different segments. The argument then goes that this differentiation is afforded by digital fabrication tools. Instead, the VoxelChair looks at a method that assembles one identical tool-path fragment, as a discrete element, into a complex and materially efficient whole.[9] This method advances both a theoretical argument about the nature of digital design as fundamentally discrete, and results in a series of efficiencies for robotic fabrication.[10] Just as the *Red and Blue Chair*, the VoxelChair is effectively an experiment with architectural syntax. Unlike an escape to the small scale, the knowledge embedded in both is actually a product of large-scale thinking and contributes to a wider architectural discourse. It is important to realise that in examples such as these, the large-scale informs the small-scale, and not the other way around as Leach argues.

Although the *Red and Blue Chair* is a piece of architectural research, and not particularly comfortable, it did enter the market as a product. Similarly, the VoxelChair 1.0 is now being commercialised as a product for market. To do so, Nagami Design, a large-scale 3D-printing startup, was founded to scale up the production. As another spin-off from this architectural research, a software product is being developed that gives users access to large-scale robotic printing.

RETHINKING ARCHITECTURE

By iterating through small- and medium-scale prototypes, while keeping an architectural agenda in mind, emerging research practices and institutes have been able to quickly develop new insights about digital production and design. They have also started to define a new type of aesthetics, at times highly material and messy. Some of them, such as the Block Research Group, have targeted part of their research on solutions for housing in developing countries – a shift away from previous decades. I would therefore argue that it is exactly this new large-scale, research-based architecture that is rethinking architecture and poised to reboot the agenda for digital design research post the 2008 financial crisis.

The work coming out of these new research labs has another ambition than mere formal differentiation; it wants to be scaled up and applied. The types of funky formal experiments that defined the 2000s seem to now be siphoned off into 3D-printed fashion and products. There are miniature Hernan Diaz-Alonsos printed in sugar, parametric urbanism research making a comeback in the form of a 3D-printed dress, and recycled Voronoi patterns on the soles of Nike Shoes. Fashion design seems to offer a market for the kind of streamlined aesthetics that try hard to convince us that the future has arrived. While the research agendas engaged with large-scale fabrication have moved on to newer arenas, some of the experiments in this *Δ* seem to still revel in the paradigm set out by Lynn's teapots more than a decade ago.

Instead of surrendering the discipline to '3D-printed body architecture', it is research focused on large-scale digital production that offers a promising direction in which architects can also successfully experiment with smaller-scale prototypes and start to blur the boundaries of the profession. It makes more sense to understand many of the contributors to this *Δ* as part of a wider shift in architectural practice, rather than a move away from the large-scale as Leach argues. Of course, compared to the world of fashion and products, this research effort may seem frustratingly slow. As Koolhaas has pointed out, architecture is one of the last professions caught between the past and the present.[11] However, this slowness gives architecture the chance to resist superfluous hypes and trends, and engage with deeper and more fundamental questions. In the end there is only so much one can learn from a 3D-printed dress. *Δ*

Notes
1. Neil Leach, *The Anaesthetics of Architecture*, MIT Press (Cambridge, MA), 1999.
2. Jean Baudrillard, *Fatal Strategies*, Semiotext(e) (New York), 1990.
3. Neil Leach, 'There is No Such Thing as Digital Architecture', in David Gerber and Mariana Ibañez, *Paradigms in Computing: Making, Machines, and Models for Design Agency in Architecture*, Evolo Press (New York), 2015.
4. Rem Koolhaas, *Delirious New York: A Retroactive Manifesto for Manhattan*, Monacelli Press (New York), 1994, p 128 (first published in 1978).
5. Mario Carpo, *The Alphabet and the Algorithm*, MIT Press (Cambridge, MA), 2011.
6. '3D Printing and Clever Computers Could Revolutionise Construction', *The Economist*, 3 June 2017: www.economist.com/news/science-and-technology/21722820-think-spiderweb-floors-denser-skyscrapers-and-ultra-thin-bridges-3d-printing-and.
7. Greg Lynn, *Animate Form*, Princeton Architectural Press (New York), 1999.
8. Gilles Retsin, 'Discrete Assembly and Digital Materials in Architecture', in *Complexity and Simplicity, Proceedings of the 34th International Conference on Education and Research in Computer Aided Architectural Design in Europe (eCAADe)*, Vol 1, 2016, pp 143–51.
9. Gilles Retsin Gilles, Manuel Jiménez and Vicente Soler, 'Discrete Computation for Additive Manufacturing', in Achim Menges et al, *Fabricate: Rethinking Design and Construction*, UCL Press (London), 2017, pp 178–83.
10. Neil Gershenfeld has successfully argued the link between discreteness and digital production. His argument, based on the notion of digital materials, is in fact also a counter-argument to Leach's in 'There is No Such Thing as Digital Architecture'. See Neil Gershenfeld et al, 'Macrofabrication With Digital Materials: Robotic Assembly', in Achim Menges, *AD Material Synthesis: Fusing the Physical and the Computational*, September/October (no 5), 2015, pp 122–7.
11. Rem Koolhaas, *Content: Triumph of Realization*, Taschen (Cologne), 2004.

Text © 2017 John Wiley & Sons Ltd. Images: pp 126-7, 130 Courtesy Greg Lynn FORM, photo Carlo Lavatori; p 128 Gilles Retsin, photo by Reio Avaste; p 131 © Digital Building Technologies, ETH Zurich; p 132(t) © Gilles Retsin and Manuel Jiménez; p 132(b) © Bartlett School of Architecture, UCL

Paola Antonelli is a Senior Curator in the Department of Architecture and Design at the Museum of Modern Art (MoMA), as well as founding Director of Research and Development. She has curated numerous shows at MoMA and in other international institutions. She has lectured worldwide in settings ranging from peer conferences to global interdisciplinary gatherings such as the World Economic Forum in Davos, Switzerland, and has served on several international architecture and design juries. She has taught at the University of California, Los Angeles (UCLA), Harvard Graduate School of Design (GSD), and the MFA programmes of the School of Visual Arts in New York. She has a Master's degree in Architecture from the Polytechnic of Milan, and holds Honorary Doctorate degrees from the Royal College of Art (RCA) and Kingston University in London, the Art Center College of Design, Pasadena, and Pratt Institute in New York.

Francis Bitonti blends computational design with emerging technologies to usher in a new manufacturing paradigm. He is known for Dita Von Teese's 3D-printed dress and his Mutatio 3D-printed shoes for United Nude, which were featured in *Wired*, the *New York Times* and *Wall Street Journal*. His pieces are in the Cooper Hewitt, Smithsonian Design Museum in New York and the Boston Museum of Fine Arts to name a few. He was also named a 2015 Wired Innovation Fellow. He holds a Master of Architecture from Pratt Institute, and is the founder of Studio Bitonti.

Niccolò Casas is an architect and professor, and principal and founder of Niccolò Casas Architecture. He is a visiting faculty member at the Rhode Island School of Design, and a PhD candidate at the Bartlett School of Architecture, University College London (UCL). His work highlights the intersection of architecture, fashion and technology via the application of emergent digital technologies and additive manufacturing. His most recent work includes collaborations with the fashion designer Iris van Herpen for the Magnetic Motion, Hacking Infinity and Lucid haute-couture shows in Paris, and for 'The Future of Fashion is Now' exhibition at the Museum Boijmans Van Beuningen in Rotterdam.

Madeline Gannon is a multidisciplinary designer working at the intersection of art and technology. She leads ATONATON, a research studio inventing better ways to communicate with machines. In her research, she designs and implements cutting-edge tools that explore the future of digital making. Her work blends disciplinary knowledge from design, robotics and human–computer interaction to innovate at the edges of digital creativity. She is currently completing a PhD in Computational Design at Carnegie Mellon University in Pittsburgh, Pennsylvania, where she is developing techniques for digitally designing and fabricating wearables on and around the body.

Eric Goldemberg is the cofounder of MONAD Studio, a design research practice with a focus on spatial perception related to rhythmic affect. He is Associate Professor and Digital Design Coordinator at Florida International University in Miami, and the author of the book *Pulsation in Architecture* (J Ross Publishing, 2011), which highlights the range and complexity of sensations involved in constructing rhythmic ensembles. His work has been widely published, including in the *Guardian*, BBC, *Le Monde*, *New York Times*, *Forbes Magazine* and *Architectural Record*.

Julia Koerner is an award-winning designer working at the convergence of architecture, product and fashion design, specialising in additive manufacturing and robotic technology. Her work has been featured internationally in world-renowned museums, institutions and publications. She is founder and director of JK Design GmbH. Her recent collaborations have included 3D-printed fashion pieces developed with haute-couture houses for Paris Fashion Week. She is a graduate of the Architectural Association (AA) in London, and the University of Applied Arts, Vienna, and a faculty member at UCLA.

Rem D Koolhaas (not to be confused with his older uncle Rem Koolhaas, the world-famous architect) is a Dutch architect trained at the Technical University of Delft in the Netherlands. He is the Creative Director and cofounder of United Nude, which launched in 2003 with the Möbius shoe. Under his creative leadership, the firm has become a world leader in technically advanced architectural footwear. With over 10 years of experience in 3D printing, United Nude is now a regular collaborator with 3D-printing market leader 3D Systems.

Jesse Louis-Rosenberg is an artist, computer programmer and maker. In 2007 he cofounded Nervous System, where his official job title is Chief Science Officer. He is interested in how simulation techniques can be used in design, and in the creation of new kinds of fabrication machines. He studied maths at MIT, and previously worked at Gehry Technologies in building modelling and design automation.

Steven Ma is an architect, designer and professor, and founder and Chief Design Officer of Xuberance Design Co Ltd. He was recently appointed as the SCI-Arc Asia Satellite Program Director. He teaches at Tongji University College of Design and Innovation, as well as at the Guangzhou Academy of Fine Arts. A digital design pioneer, his work has been widely published and exhibited. He was previously a lead design architect at Xefirotarch in Los Angeles (2006–8) and CoopHimmelb(l)au in Vienna (2008–12). He received the American Institute of Architecture Year Award 2009 (Henry Adam Medal Prize) as well as SCI-Arc Best Graduate Thesis Project of the Year 2008. He has also conducted numerous international workshops.

Neri Oxman is an architect, designer, inventor and associate professor based at the MIT Media Lab at the Massachusetts Institute of Technology. Her Mediated Matter Group operates at the intersection of computational design, digital fabrication, materials science and synthetic biology, and applies that knowledge to design across scales and disciplines. Her work is included in the permanent collections at the Museum of Modern Art (MoMA) in New York, San Francisco Museum of Modern Art (SFMOMA), Centre Pompidou and the Smithsonian Institution, among others. Awards include the Vilcek Prize in Design, BSA Women in Design Award and Silicon Valley Visionary Award. Her work has resulted in more than 100 scientific papers and patents, and her innovations have received recognition at the World Economic Forum where she is part of the Expert Network, and the White House.

Ronald Rael is an associate professor and the Eva Li Memorial Chair at the University of California, Berkeley. He directs the printFARM Laboratory (print Facility for Architecture, Research and Materials), and holds a joint appointment in the Department of Architecture, the College of Environmental Design and the Department of Art Practice. He is a partner in Rael San Fratello and Emerging Objects with Virginia San Fratello. He is the author of *Borderwall as Architecture: A Manifesto for the US–Mexico Boundary* (University of California Press, 2017), *Earth Architecture* (Princeton Architectural Press, 2010) and the forthcoming book with San Fratello, *Emerging Objects: A 3D Printing Cookbook for Architecture* (Princeton Architectural Press, 2018).

Gilles Retsin is the founder of Gilles Retsin Architecture, a young award-winning London-based architecture and design practice. He is a lecturer at the Bartlett School of Architecture, UCL, Programme Director of the MArch Architectural Design and codirector of the Design Computation Lab. His work has been acquired by the Centre Pompidou in Paris, and he has exhibited internationally, for example in the Museum of Art and Design in New York, Vitra Design Museum in Weil-am-Rhein, Design Exchange Toronto and the Zaha Hadid Gallery in London. He has lectured and acted as a guest critic in numerous universities. He graduated from the AA in London. Prior to founding his own practice, he worked in Switzerland as a project architect with Christian Kerez, and in London with Kokkugia.

Jessica Rosenkrantz is an artist, designer and programmer. In 2007 she cofounded Nervous System, where she currently works as Creative Director. Her work explores how simulations of natural processes can be used in design and coupled with digital fabrication to create one-of-a-kind customised products. She is a lecturer in the Department of Architecture at the Massachusetts Institute of Technology (MIT). She studied biology and architecture at MIT and at Harvard GSD. Nervous System's designs have been featured in a wide range of publications, including the *Guardian*, *New York Times* and *Wired*, and are part of the permanent collections of the Cooper Hewitt, Smithsonian Design Museum and MoMA in New York.

Virginia San Fratello is an architect, artist and educator. She is an Associate Professor in the Department of Design at San Jose State University in California, and Director of the Interior Design Program. She recently won the International Interior Design Educator of the Year Award, and her creative practice, Rael San Fratello (with Ronald Rael), was named an Emerging Voice by the Architectural League of New York. She is also a winner of the *Metropolis* magazine Next Generation Design Competition. Her work with Rael has been published widely, including in the *New York Times*, *Wired*, *Domus*, *PRAXIS* and *Interior Design Magazine*, and has been recognised by several institutions including MoMA and the Cooper Hewitt, Smithsonian Design Museum.

Patrik Schumacher is principal of Zaha Hadid Architects, and has been leading the firm since Zaha's passing in March 2016. He joined the practice in 1988. In 1996 he founded the Design Research Laboratory (DRL) at the AA, where he continues to teach. Over the last 20 years he has contributed over 100 articles to architectural journals and anthologies. Since 2007 he has been promoting 'parametricism' as an epochal style for the 21st century. He is the author of *The Autopoiesis of Architecture* (John Wiley & Sons, 2010/12), and Guest-Editor of ◬ *Parametricism 2.0: Rethinking Architecture's Agenda for the 21st Century* (March/April 2016), emphasising the societal relevance of this style.

Kyle von Hasseln is a graduate of Middlebury College in Vermont, with a focus on biology. He earned a Master's degree at SCI-Arc, where together with his partner Liz von Hasseln their 'Phantom Geometry' 3D-printing research won the inaugural Frank Gehry Prize for best graduate thesis. Together they cofounded The Sugar Lab, a design and technology research firm that was acquired by 3D Systems in 2013, where Kyle is currently Culinary Technology Director. Their work has appeared in numerous publications including the *New York Times*, *Washington Post*, *Dwell*, *Popular Mechanics*, *Time Magazine*, *The Atlantic*, *Wired*, *TechCrunch*, the Discovery Channel and the BBC.

What is *Architectural Design*?

Founded in 1930, *Architectural Design* (Δ) is an influential and prestigious publication. It combines the currency and topicality of a newsstand journal with the rigour and production qualities of a book. With an almost unrivalled reputation worldwide, it is consistently at the forefront of cultural thought and design.

Each title of Δ is edited by an invited Guest-Editor, who is an international expert in the field. Renowned for being at the leading edge of design and new technologies, Δ also covers themes as diverse as architectural history, the environment, interior design, landscape architecture and urban design.

Provocative and pioneering, Δ inspires theoretical, creative and technological advances. It questions the outcome of technical innovations as well as the far-reaching social, cultural and environmental challenges that present themselves today.

For further information on Δ, subscriptions and purchasing single issues see:

http://onlinelibrary.wiley.com/journal/10.1002/%28ISSN%291554-2769

Volume 86 No 6
ISBN 978 1119 099581

Volume 87 No 1
ISBN 978 1119 099581

Volume 87 No 2
ISBN 978 1119 162131

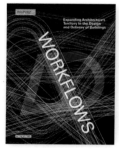

Volume 87 No 3
ISBN 978 1119 317845

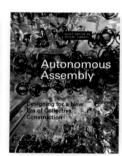

Volume 87 No 4
ISBN 978 1119 102359

Volume 87 No 5
ISBN 978 1119 152644

How to Subscribe
With 6 issues a year, you can subscribe to Δ (either print, online or through the Δ App for iPad)

Institutional subscription
£275 / US$516
print or online

Institutional subscription
£330 / US$620
combined print and online

Personal-rate subscription
£128 / US$201
print and iPad access

Student-rate subscription
£84 / US$129
print only

Δ App for iPad
6-issue subscription:
£44.99 / US$64.99
Individual issue:
£9.99 / US$13.99

To subscribe to print or online
E: cs-journals@wiley.com

Americas
E: cs-journals@wiley.com
T: +1 781 388 8598
or +1 800 835 6770
(toll free in the USA & Canada)

Europe, Middle East and Africa
E: cs-journals@wiley.com
T: +44 (0) 1865 778315

Asia Pacific
E: cs-journals@wiley.com
T: +65 6511 8000

Japan (for Japanese-speaking support)
E: cs-japan@wiley.com
T: +65 6511 8010
or 005 316 50 480
(toll-free)

Visit our Online Customer Help available in 7 languages at www.wileycustomerhelp.com/ask